TWAYNE'S WORLD AUTHORS SERIES

A Survey of the World's Literature

Sylvia E. Bowman, Indiana University

GENERAL EDITOR

FRANCE

Maxwell A. Smith, Guerry Professor of French, Emeritus
The University of Chattanooga
Former Visiting Professor in Modern Languages
The Florida State University

EDITOR

Henri Michaux

TWAS 465

Henri Michaux

HENRI MICHAUX

By VIRGINIA A. LA CHARITÉ
University of Kentucky

TWAYNE PUBLISHERS
A DIVISION OF G. K. HALL & CO., BOSTON

Library of Congress Cataloging in Publication Data

La Charité, Virginia A
Henri Michaux.

(Twayne's world authors series ; TWAS 465 : France)
Bibliography: p. 141–44
Includes index.
1. Michaux, Henri, 1899–   —Criticism and inter-
pretation.
PQ2625.I2Z68   848'.9'1209   77–5325
ISBN 0–8057–6302–3

For Raymond

Contents

About the Author

Preface

Chronology

1. The Field of Conscience   15

2. Terrains of Existence   21

3. Plume and the Serenity of Night   39

4. Eureka! Liberation of the Imagination   54

5. To Paint a Poem   76

6. The Magic of Motion   93

7. The Vastness of Morpho-Creation   107

8. The Design of Destiny   121

    Notes and References   135

    Selected Bibliography   141

    Index   145

About the Author

Virginia A. La Charité received her A.B. degree from the College of William and Mary, her M.A. and Ph.D. degrees from the University of Pennsylvania. She has taught at the College of William and Mary, the University of North Carolina at Chapel Hill, and since 1969 at the University of Kentucky, where she has also served as the president of Phi Beta Kappa and the Chairman of the Comparative Literature Program.

Professor La Charité has held a Fulbright grant and several university research fellowships. She is the author of *The Poetics and the Poetry of René Char* and the co-editor and co-translator of *Bonaventure des Périers's Novel Pastimes and Merry Tales*. In addition, she has published essays on a variety of topics in *PMLA, Modern Language Review, Romance Notes, French Review, Nineteenth-Century French Studies, Symposium, Studies in Philology,* and *Studi Francesi*. She is the co-founder and co-editor of *French Forum* and *French Forum Monographs*.

Preface

Henri Michaux is a protean figure whose work defies classification. It *is*, just as he is — with all the inherent spirality contained therein. To enter Michaux's universe is to leave one's own. As Proust once wrote, the role of artists is to give us another world view, for, without one, each of us is limited to his own vision of things. Michaux, a composite creator in whose world all facets of human endeavor come together, offers access to a multiple perspective of the creative process which, in its absolute generic unity, resists definition.

The very essence of Michaux's work lies in its balance of contradictions, dilemmas, changes, and paradoxes. At times, he is a poet in the most elevated sense of the word. On other occasions, he is a practitioner of magic, a rebel, a scandalizer, a defiler, a scorner. From one perspective, he is a painter whose work equals the best that modern art has produced, and his paintings are shown internationally. Yet, some of his texts and paintings tend to present him as a tortured soul who fails to synthesize Gidian *disponibilité* and Sartrian *engagement*. It is certainly admissible to see Michaux as a pessimist, a skeptic, a critic, a satirist, a humorist, a destroyer of mores. . . even a tragic clown whose revolt against the absurd always ends in a stalemate.

Were I to single out the one term which best describes the complexity of Michaux the artist, I would unhesitatingly choose *poet*. Poet as defined first by Plato and second by Rimbaud. Poet as creator. Poet as the generative source of human perfectibility. At a time when there seem to be two opposing camps of poets and their critics — those who advocate Poetry as the Absolute of existence and those who deny the existence of poetry through the hostile stance of autonomous transcription or *mécriture* — there is Henri Michaux, who denies identification with either camp and yet participates in both through the reconciling force of the poetic rhythm of expression. Hence, the paradox within Michaux's artistic conversion of inner human desires into reality is — because of that paradox — realistic, constructive, and humanly satisfying.

Michaux believes that man has the potential to achieve self-realization through his own tools: prose, painting, music, science, religion, verse, humor, magic, drugs, dreams, poetry.

Thus, the problem in approaching Michaux is to discern how the man, the painter, and the poet are bound together in a creative vision of unity; for his multilateral work does indeed present a confusing labyrinth to the reader. In an effort to erect guideposts through the maze of his multifaceted artistic adventure, I have followed a loosely chronological format, one which attempts to trace Michaux's own linear journey of expansion-contraction-expansion-retraction, which he notes in *Emergences-Résurgences*. Like a spiral, his work increases in momentum, widens, recoils, only to open outward again; as each ring of the spiral uncoils, a coherent whole is glimpsed. In order to show Michaux's emergence-resurgence pattern in operation, I have combined works which form a single spiral. Consequently, the combinations at times cut across both chronological lines and volume arrangement; for example, *Mes Propriétés* appears with *Qui je fus* and not with *La Nuit remue, Un Barbare en Asie* is treated with the three works of *Ailleurs,* and the drug texts have been grouped together.

Because I have chosen to adopt Michaux's architecture of the spiral, I have also followed his dictum of *passage.* In order to present the vortex of his intertextuality, some of his works are examined as only one part of a ring of the coil, most notably *Ailleurs,* which has fascinated many readers, but which I have placed in the perspective of the ring of the imagination.

Since Michaux's adventure is a continuing one, this study ends with *Face à ce qui se dérobe* (1975), and, like any work which accepts the challenge of studying a living writer, it is perforce incomplete. No doubt, other rings of the spiral are emerging and will surge forth soon, and there are most likely those who detect different rings than the ones which the chapters of this book discern. I earnestly hope so, for the Michaux universe, if it is anything at all, represents a challenge to the reader to enter as he will, but, in entering, to be prepared to become the architect of his own resurgence.

Chronology

1899   May 24: Henri-Eugène-Guislain Michaux born in Namur, Belgium.

1906-   Studies in Flemish, Latin, French, music, literature, sci-
1919   ences, medicine.

1920   First sea voyages: Germany (Bremen), Holland (Rotter-dam), United States (New York, Norfolk, Newport News, Savannah), South America (Rio de Janeiro, Buenos Aires).

1921   Marseilles.

1922   Publication of first texts: "Cas de folie circulaire" (*Le Disque Vert*) and "Chronique de l'aiguilleur" (*Ecrits du Nord*). Renounces Belgium and moves to Paris.

1923   Publication in Belgium of first volumes: *Les Rêves et la jambe; Fables des origines.*

1923-   Friendships with Jules Supervielle and Jean Paulhan; dis-
1925   covery of art and artists: Klee, Ernst, Chirico. Contributor to *Cahiers du Sud, Commerce, Bifur.*

1927   Publication of *Qui je fus,* first volume published in France. Departure for Ecuador.

1928   South America, mainly in Quito, Ecuador, with Alfredo Gangotena.

1929   Return to Paris. *Ecuador; Mes Propriétés.* Death of both parents. Trips to Italy, Turkey, North Africa.

1930   *Un Certain Plume; Le Drame des constructeurs.*

1930-   Trip to Asia: India, Ceylon, Malaya, Indonesia, China,
1931   Korea, Japan. Discovery of Chinese painting.

1933   *Un Barbare en Asie.*

1935   *La Nuit remue.*

1936   *Entre centre et absence; Voyage en Grande Garabagne.*

1937   First painting exhibition.

1938   *Plume précédé de Lointain intérieur.* Editorial board of *Hermès.*

1939   *Peintures.* Trip to Brazil. Ends association with *Hermès.*

1940- Moves from Paris to Saint-Antonin, then to Lavandou.
1941 Marriage.
1941 *Au pays de La Magie.*
1942 *Arbre des Tropiques.*
1943 Returns to Paris. *Exorcismes.*
1944 *Labyrinthes; Le Lobe des monstres.* Death of his brother.
1945 *Epreuves, exorcismes; Liberté d'action.* His wife contracts tuberculosis. First edition of *L'Espace du dedans.*
1946 *Peintures et dessins; Ici, Poddema; Apparitions.*
1947 Trip to Egypt and other voyages of convalescence.
1948 *Ailleurs; Meidosems.* Death of his wife from burns in a fire. *Nous deux encore.*
1949 *La Vie dans les plis; Poésie pour pouvoir.*
1950 First edition of *Passages; Arriver à se réveiller; Tranches de savoir suivi du Secret de la situation politique.*
1951 *Mouvements.* Begins to write less and paint more.
1952 *Nouvelles de l'étranger.*
1954 *Face aux verrous.* First exhibition of ink drawings.
1955 Becomes naturalized French citizen.
1956 *Misérable Miracle; Quatre Cents Hommes en croix.* First exhibition of mescaline drawings. Begins to participate in international art exhibitions (New York, Rome).
1957 *L'Infini turbulent.* Loss of use of right hand and training of left hand.
1959 *Paix dans les brisements.*
1960 Einaudi award at Venice.
1961 *Connaissance par les gouffres.*
1962 *Vents et poussières.*
1963 Revised edition of *Passages;* definitive edition of *Plume précédé de Lointain intérieur.* Film, "Images du monde," with Duvivier.
1964 Revised edition of *L'Infini turbulent.*
1965 Refuses Le Grand Prix National des Lettres.
1966 *Les Grandes Epreuves de l'esprit et les innombrables petites;* revised edition of *L'Espace du dedans.* Exhibition of "dessins de désagrégation."
1967 *Vers la complétude;* revised edition of *Ailleurs.*
1969 *Façons d'endormi, façons d'éveillé.*
1971 *Poteaux d'angle.*

Chronology

1972   *Emergences-Résurgences; En rêvant à partir de peintures énigmatiques;* revised edition with Addenda of *Misérable Miracle.*

1973   *Moments: Traversées du temps.*

1974   *Par la voie des rythmes.*

1975   *Face à ce qui se dérobe.*

1976   Exhibition at the Fondation Maeght.

CHAPTER 1

The Field of Conscience

S IGNES, śymboles, élans, chutes, départs, rapports, discordances, tout
y est pour rebondir, pour chercher, pour plus loin, pour autre chose.
Entre eux, sans s'y fixer, l'auteur poussa sa vie (Signs, symbols, bursts,
spills, departures, connections, discordances, it's all there for rebounding,
for seeking, for pushing ahead, for something else. Among them, without
settling in, the author thrust his life, *PLI*, p. 220).[1]

Poet, painter, traveler, fabulist, journalist, *prosateur,* amateur psychol-
ogist, sociologist, adventurer, linguist, dramatist, critic, dreamer, essayist,
philosopher, musician — Henri Michaux defies classification. With
countless interests and many talents, he remains aloof from all literary
schools and movements; indeed, his search for total expression demands a
cosmopolitanism that does away with all boundaries and national limits,
including those of language. Belgian by birth, Spanish and German in an-
tecedents, and French by election, Michaux's first verbal mode is Flemish,
but his chosen written mode is French. Even on the physical plane, he defies description; right-handed by nature, left-handed by training. Versatile
and indefatigable, Michaux's life and works represent and illustrate *hom-
misme,* self-realization through the abolition of limitation.

Henri Michaux[2] was born in Namur and raised in Brussels.
Owing to delicate health, he was sent to the country to attend
boarding school at Putte-Grasheide for five years. Returning to
Brussels in 1911, he undertook the study of Latin at a Jesuit school,
where he also showed interest in music and first discovered the autonomy and force of words in the dictionary. During the five years
that Brussels was occupied by the German army, Michaux continued to widen his intellectual horizons: French, literatures of various
countries, Saints' lives, the profane and the mundane, the exotic
and the strange, including the group known as "Jeune Belgique."
Having obtained his Baccalaureate in 1916, he devoted the next two
years to reading widely, deeply, and often in the realm of the

bizarre, for the University was closed because of the Occupation; once the University reopened, he enrolled as a medical student for one year. Abandoning medicine and formal education, he contemplated entering the Benedictine order, but his father refused to give his approval.

By 1920, at age 21 Michaux had crossed literary and linguistic frontiers and was well-versed in the disparate fields of science and religion, which admits no geographical boundaries. International in mind and spirit through his readings and studies, he set out on the first of his many trips to explore the world. His first voyage was as a sailor on a five-masted schooner at Boulogne-sur-Mer; at Rotterdam, he signed on the *Victorieux*, a ten-ton vessel, and made his own discovery of the New World: New York, Norfolk, Newport News, Savannah, Rio de Janeiro, Buenos Aires. His easy and close friendship with the crew of the *Victorieux* led him to join them in leaving the ship in Rio, thus avoiding the shipwreck which occurred 20 days later. In 1921, Michaux landed in Marseilles, but, after holding several menial jobs, he finally returned to Brussels in 1922. There he read Lautréamont for the first time and began to write for the journal, *Le Disque Vert,* which had just been founded by Franz Hellenz. Later, disenchanted with his family's view of him as a failure and not content with his literary efforts, he permanently left Brussels and moved to Paris.

Michaux's search for a vocation which might also be his avocation and his desire to be international — free from all ties and limitations — even led him to a distaste for his own name, but all attempts at finding a pseudonym failed. Still looking for an independent identity, he remained apart from the various literary groups in Paris. Encouraged by Jules Supervielle and Jean Paulhan, he wrote for journals such as *Cahiers du Sud, Commerce,* and *Bifur,* while his first two works, *Les Rêves et la jambe (Dreams and the Leg)* and *Fables des origines (Fables on Origins)* were published in Belgium in 1923 and were relatively unnoticed. Through Paulhan, Michaux was introduced to the young avant-garde of the Parisian artistic scene of the 1920's, especially the Surrealists; but true to his renouncement of an imposed identity and existence, he never became even a fringe member of this or any other group. Rather, his acquaintance with the Surrealists and others led him to a major discovery, painting, which he had previously detested. His fascination with the expressive power of plastic art and its non-reliance on the fixed form of language in turn caused him to seek out Paul Klee, Max Ernst, Georges Chirico, André Masson, Salvador Dali. With Paulhan's help, Michaux published *Qui je fus (Who I Was)* in 1927; this volume is not only his first work published in France, but also his first work taken seriously by a literary audience. *Qui je fus* captures in its title Michaux's 28-year effort to divorce himself from the limits of familial, linguistic, and cultural determination and to assert his own independent identity.

Attracted to the Equatorian poet, Alfredo Gangotena, Michaux went with him to Ecuador and spent a year with him in Quito. Out of this experience came the journal *Ecuador*, which was quickly followed by *Mes Propriétés,* the volume which contains Michaux's first extensive use of verse texts. In 1929, the death of both parents within ten days of each other precipitated an internal crisis; travels to Turkey, Italy, and North Africa — what Michaux describes as "voyages d'expatriation" — were undertaken in an effort to divest himself of the cultural influences remaining within his psychological framework. The resulting distance brought about through travel is reflected in the creation of his first well-known fictional character, Plume, in *Un Certain Plume* (1930) and in the writing of his first play, *Le Drame des constructeurs (The Builders' Drama,* 1930). 1930-1931 marks Michaux's longest trip: India, Ceylon, Malaya, Indonesia, China, Korea, Japan. The immediate result of his Asian experience was *Un Barbare en Asie (A Barbarian in Asia,* 1933), but the impact of his encounter with non-Western culture, particularly in the area of painting, continues to the very present: "L'Asie, maintenant loin, revient, me submergeant par moments, par longs moments" ("Asia, now difficult to remember, comes back, submerging me at times, for long periods of time," *E-R,* p. 17). The Asian trip was quickly followed by a visit to Lisbon in 1932 and trips to Montevideo and Buenos Aires in 1935, the same year that *La Nuit remue (Night on the Move)* appeared.

By 1935, Michaux's Western childhood had been fundamentally altered by non-European influences and discoveries. The inner voyage of the adolescent into the world of books and the outer voyages of the young adult into other modes of existence combined to open paths to new voyages for the mature man: Michaux rapidly wrote his first imaginary travelogue, *Voyage en Grande Garabagne (Trip to Great Garabagne,* 1936), undertook his first exploration of inner space in *Entre centre et absence (Between Center and Absence,*

1936), and held his first art exhibition at the Galerie Pierre in Paris (1937).

Close association with the journal *Hermès* from 1938-1939 opened up yet another path to explore: the relationship of mysticism to poetry and philosophy. With the publication of *Peintures* (*Paintings,* 1939), which represents his first attempt to bring together poetry and painting, and, after another trip to Brazil, Michaux turned to the examination of magic as a creative force of expression. *Au pays de La Magie (In the Land of Magic)* in 1941 was quickly followed by *Exorcismes* (1943), *Labyrinthes* (1944), and *Le Lobe des monstres* (*The Monsters' Lobes,* 1944), which are in turn collected into *Epreuves, exorcismes* (*Trials, Exorcisms,* 1945). In a way, these works stand as Michaux's literal use of verbal magic to exorcise the German Occupation of Paris, which marked his second personal experiencing of a foreign occupation.

Moving first to Saint-Antonin and then to Lavandou, where he married, Michaux returned to occupied Paris in 1943 and undertook the preparation of his first anthology, *L'Espace du dedans (The Space Within),* whose publication in 1945 along with *Liberté d'action (Freedom of Action)* followed two personal tragedies, the death of his brother (1944) and his wife's contracting tuberculosis. Michaux's publications in 1946 were those written during the war years: *Peintures et dessins (Paintings and Drawings),* which is an expanded edition of *Peintures; Ici, Poddema (Here, Poddema),* which continues the voyage into the imagination launched by *Voyage en Grande Garabagne;* and *Apparitions,* which reflects his interest in the dream world.

In order to help his wife convalesce, Michaux took her on trips throughout 1947. In 1948, he published his imaginary voyages, *Ailleurs (Elsewhere)* and *Meidosems;* in the latter, he tried his hand for the first time at the art of lithography, for the work combines poetical analysis of a mythical culture and lithographs of these imaginary people. But 1948 was also marked by the tragic death of his wife from burns received in a fire which was all the more painful for Michaux because his wife was on the verge of recovery from tuberculosis. His grief and love are recorded in his beautiful homage to her: *Nous deux encore (Still the Two of Us),* published in the same year. By 1949, death had severed all of Michaux's familial ties; turning away more and more from poetry, he produced in 1950 the collected edition of his essays, *Passages,* the self-study *Arriver à se réveiller (Trying to Wake Up),* and the aphoristic *Tranches de savoir suivi du Secret de la situation politique (Slices of Knowledge followed by The Secret of the Political Situation).*

In 1951, *Mouvements* heralded a decrease in Michaux's actual writing and marked his increasing devotion to painting. Although *Nouvelles de l'étranger (News from Abroad)* was published in 1952 and the collected volume *Face aux verrous (Facing the Locks)* appeared in 1954, these works put an end to a rather productive cycle of writing. From this period on, written works have appeared less and less frequently, while there has scarcely been a year in which there has not been a major art exhibition.

Shortly after the publication of *Face aux verrous,* Michaux turned to drug experimentation. In 1955, he became a naturalized French citizen and returned to his earlier scientific interest in medicine. Always intrigued by the psyche and the inner space of man's existence, as well as his identity and creativity, Michaux began a deeper inner voyage than any he had previously undertaken. In the same way that he had made his written and plastic expression compatible, he set out to bridge the gap between literature and science. It should be noted at the outset that Michaux's use of drugs does not fall within the literary lineage that began with Nerval and continued through Baudelaire, Rimbaud, the Surrealists, and others. Rather, Michaux's interest is impersonal, detached, objective; he does not experiment in order to create, but rather to discover and dissect the source of creation in man's inner space. Never *engagé,* always *désengagé,* his powers of observation were clinically applied to self-study and analysis in *Misérable Miracle* (1956), *L'Infini turbulent (The Turbulent Infinite,* 1957), *Paix dans les brisements (Peace in Debris,* 1959), *Connaissance par les gouffres (Learning through Despair,* 1961), *Les Grandes Epreuves de l'esprit et les innombrables petites (Great Trials of the Mind and Countless Minor Ones,* 1966). Even *Vents et poussières (Winds and Dust,* 1962) and *Vers la complétude (Toward Fulfillment,* 1966) are related to his drug experiences and experimentation. Yet these same "drug" years were accompanied by three important non-drug related events: Michaux's painting received international acclaim and was shown world-wide; having lost the use of his right hand, he managed to train and develop his left to an equal degree of dexterity and reliability; and he revised and republished the works that were beginning to be considered his major literary contributions —

Ailleurs (1961 and 1967), *La Nuit remue* (1961 and 1967), *Plume précédé de Lointain intérieur* (1963 and 1967), *L'Espace du dedans* (1966), *Un Barbare en Asie* (1967), *Face aux verrous* (1967), *Ecuador* (1968).

In 1965, Michaux received the Grand Prix National des Lettres, but his personal motto of independence led him to refuse it.

While it is impossible at this writing to judge accurately the nature of Michaux's decade of drug experimentation and its effect on his creativity, it can be stated that this particular period in his total artistry reveals two significant discoveries. First, science and artistic endeavor are not irreconcilable, as witnessed by the drawings which accompany many of the texts and as expressed by the dominance of poetry in the commentaries (before, during, and after the use of a drug) which describe the experience. The most notable example is perhaps *Paix dans les brisements,* which consists of a prose commentary, a free verse poem, and a drawing, and which demands all three media for the full expression (and comprehension) of the experience. Second, since the decade of drug experimentation, Michaux has produced no new poetry in a formal sense. *Façons d'endormi, façons d'éveillé* (*Sleeping Modes, Waking Modes,* 1969) pursues the study of dreams as nightmares and reverie in the same detached clinical manner that characterizes most of his texts related to drugs; *Poteaux d'angle* (*Corner Posts,* 1971) is a collection of aphorisms; *Emergences-Résurgences* (1972) is an examination of his evolution as a painter and experimenter with lines and signs; *Moments: Traversées du temps* (*Moments: Passages of Time,* 1973) reorders previously published poetry; *Par la voie des rythmes* (*Along the Path of Rhythm,* 1974) continues the figures of *Mouvements* but is singular in its total omission of the printed word. *Face à ce qui se dérobe* (*Facing What is Disappearing,* 1975), the last work considered in this study, is a prose résumé of the voyage first undertaken in *Qui je fus,* but one which continues to haunt its creator and to fascinate the reader.

CHAPTER 2

Terrains of Existence

TROUVER son terrain, le terrain pour l'exercice d'une vie, d'une autre vie en instance, d'une nouvelle vie à accomplir, *hic et nunc,* une vie qui n'était pas là avant (Find one's own terrain, the terrain for the exercise of a life, of another expectant life, a new life to be accomplished, *here and now,* a life which wasn't there before, *E-R,* p. 74).

Henri Michaux's early publications reveal the same concerns of his later works: problems of communication, the absurdity of the self as a single unit, the subconscious as a means of knowledge, psychoanalysis, the deformation of shapes, the mechanism of things, the exploration of the fantastic to explain the everyday. His first work, *Les Rêves et la jambe (Dreams and the Leg,* 1923), deals with incommunicability and physical fragmentation. In this volume, subtitled "A Philosophical and Literary Essay," Michaux first finds expression in the style of an "awakened man" ("homme réveillé"), for "Le rêve est la rentrée de l'inconscient dans le conscient" ("Dreaming is the penetration of the subconscious into the conscious"). Dreams are man's interior reality, his inner space, while exterior physical reality is captured by the leg of the title. Upon waking from sleep, the dreamer feels dismembered; in his first attempt at reorientation in outer space, he discovers a limb, a part, rather than a whole: "Rêve: un grand morceau d'homme qui dort et un petit morceau qui est éveillé" ("Dream: a large piece of the man who sleeps and a little bit of the one who has awakened," p. 11). The familiar physical self is consequently known through the experience of being disjointed. The whole self ignores its parts and is scarcely aware of them unless some experience unleashes a sudden emotion concerning a particular part of the body. The dream, because it disorients and distorts the conscious real, gives value to the experience of the conscious, a value that would in all

21

probability have remained undiscovered except through the instrument of the subconscious, here the dream.

While this fascination with the dream and the subconscious may seem to border on Surrealism, Michaux does not share the Surrealist interest in the processes of the subconscious. On the contrary, he views the dream as a means of access to a terrain of man's existence: inner space which alone can explain — deductively and logically — how a self, a personality, is born and gains meaning. At no time does Michaux fully give himself over to the subconscious, just as he never adopts Surrealist practices such as automatic writing and dream recitation. For Michaux, the dream has a purpose; its utility lies in the experience of awakening: "Caractère du rêve: insensibilité! Anaffectivité. . . Emotion générale: éveil" ("Characteristic of the dream: insensitivity! Anaffectivity. . . General emotion: awakening"). Only what is felt, experienced, possessed, is of value. And since man only becomes aware of himself through the disorientation of an inner space experience, such as the dream, the role of literature becomes one of deformation in order to force the reader into greater self-awareness: "La déformation seule intéresse la littérature" ("Only deformation is of interest to literature"). The writer is like a train switchman, as captured by Michaux's 1922 "Chronique de l'aiguilleur" ("Switchman's Chronicle"); he switches man from track to track, terrain to terrain, in an effort to take on verbally the same nature of reentry that the dream is able to achieve when the sleeper awakens: displacement so that the component parts may be known. Disengagement of the familiar — the leg, for example — and loss of shape are hallmarks of Michaux's repudiation of the world of reproduction; and, by 1923, his fascination with the problem of man's formation and subsequent formulation was established.

In his second work, *Fables des origines (Fables on Origins),* which was also published in 1923, Michaux takes up such diverse topics as anthropology, humor, God, divination, instincts, animals, painting. All the subjects he examines are related to his departure from a normal description of things, as in the chapter title, "L'Homme qui mange son fils" ("The Man Who Eats His Son"). Michaux's fictions consistently evoke, if not provoke, emotion, the general character of consciousness, the terrain of existence.

Shortly after the publication of *Les Rêves et la jambe* and *Fables des origines,* Michaux lauded Charlie Chaplin for his comic astuteness in projecting inner desires into physical acts and criticized André Breton's "Poisson soluble" on the grounds that automatic writing is emotionless and literally impossible since the hand is incapable of following the speed of thought. Moreover, Michaux, ever the rationalist who uses the marvelous as a way of constructing a meaning in life, takes exception to the term *surrealism* and proposes instead two other terms: *Introrealism* and *Extrarealism.* While Michaux himself never opts for either *intro-* or *extra-* realism (much less *sur*-realism), it is significant that (1) he constantly refers to the awakened state, the conscious, that (2) he emphasizes the concrete, rational, and knowable as the base of a form of realism, and that (3) he perceives that the Surrealist marriage between the dream and the awakened state is not a genuine union, not a suprareality, but an alliance in which one is either *intro* (dreaming) or *extra* (awake). For Michaux, there is no salvation on the terrain of either the subconscious or the imagination. There is only the terrain of the reentered conscience, emotion. Hence, when he moved to Paris, he remained aloof from the Surrealist writers. While he had certain affinities with Surrealism (dream, marvelous, subconscious), he was first and foremost a rationalist for whom experiences of inner space must be measured in terms of the value they bring to human existence.

On the other hand, Michaux's early (pre-Parisian) work is hostile in its view of reproductive creation, a hostility shared by Surrealist painters. His interest was not in existence as it is, but as it emerges: "La lettre tue, l'esprit vivifie" ("The letter kills, the spirit vitalizes," "Manuscrit trouvé dans une poche" — "Manuscript Found in a Pocket," 1923). The force of life, as opposed to its actual form, is the common thread which links Michaux's early works together and ties them to his later volumes as well. Throughout *Les Rêves et la jambe* and *Fables des origines,* he confronted the problem of formation and its formulation. In "Chronique de l'aiguilleur," he attacked art as mimicry, for it is cut off from its roots and dying of techniques. Man has lost his expression; the machine age of scientific technology has produced images and ideas in assembly-line fashion. Hence, Surrealist artistic experiments appealed to the young Michaux who was seeking new ways of expression which would serve in his acquisition of self-knowledge.

The freedom from form captured by the avant-garde painters in Paris in the 1920's attracted Michaux. By 1925, he was familiar with the ateliers of Klee, Masson, Dali, Ernst, and had begun his own experiments with plastic art. Michaux's earliest extant adventures into non-verbal media date from 1925[1] and are not designs or sketches but "taches": formless, shapeless explosions of energy on paper: "Né, élevé, instruit dans un milieu et une culture uniquement du 'verbal' je peins *pour me déconditionner*" ("Born, reared, and educated in a uniquely 'verbal' milieu and culture, I paint *in order to decondition myself,*" E-R, p. 9). Michaux's desire and effort to divest himself of established modes of expression and his interest in the emergence of life (as opposed to the fact of the existence of life) provide the terrain for his first French volume, *Qui je fus,* composed between 1924 and 1927.

I *Separation*

Qui je fus (*Who I Was,* 1927) contains in germ form the various artistic adventures which Michaux has undertaken. In this volume of prose and free verse, he openly declares his war on form, externalizes inner conflicts, and confronts the problem of formation. As the title indicates, *Qui je fus* is the autobiography of a poet; for Michaux's first terrain of exploration is always the self: "Il faut toujours en revenir à l'observation de soi, comme à la matière première la mieux observable, la plus vaste, la plus souvent vérifiable, la plus permanente, malgré tout son instable, la moins capable de duper longtemps du tout au tout" ("We always have to come back to self-observation, because it is the best observable raw material, the vastest, the most often verifiable, the most permanent, despite all its instability, the least capable of duping us entirely for long," *P,* p. 106).

Divided into ten parts, the first section is a dialogue in prose from which the volume takes its title, "Qui je fus." The singular *I* in the present resents being forced to write about things, while the plural *who-I-was* insists that he work in a regular fashion in order to prolong the influences of the past, and, consequently, its existence. The composite societal figure, *who-I-was,* is divided into three philosophical forms: first, the Materialist who places emphasis on description, the intellect, and science for the expression of the what and why of things; second, the Redemptorist who insists that only the proper spiritual attitude controls certain sensations and thoughts; third, the Skeptic who is convinced that there is no

need for change and exploration because imperfection characterizes all experience. In addition, all three representatives of society
confess that their motive in attempting to cling to the *I* of the
present is their desire not to die. These inner forces of past formation (medical studies, Jesuit education, readings, travel, and family) demand that the writer, *I*, write philosophy and theses about
them, while *I* prefers to create and invent a novel. Tension between
form (the plural *who-I-was*) and force (*I*) is a conflict of past versus
present and future. In "Enigmes," the second section, confrontation with the past continues: *I* was a mimic, a descendant of a bour-
geois family, a wit laughed at for his quick use of words, a dreamer;
when *I* imagined, *I* was active and had the immediate experience of
adventure. The *I* in the present is to become the judge of what kinds
of experiences were of value and pleasure.

In the 12 subsections of "Partages de l'homme" ("Man's Inheri-
tance"), the *I* in the present is a seeker (and "chercheur" remains a
key term for Michaux), not a finder, and this attitude also characterizes his subsequent writings. In brief, the 12 "shares" disclose
glimpses of possibilities of getting outside the self: "Les évasions
vers où, et n'importe où son désir le poussait" ("Escapes toward
whatever and wherever his desire pushed him," *QJF,* p. 27). The
problem is to see the whole space that is the man of bone (and
"L'homme d'os" is favored over a man of flesh because the hard
substance of bone endures while flesh changes more rapidly); it is
the body which assassinates the soul. Hence, while man physically
falls from family to school to profession, from age to age, activity
does not warm the inner self and physical fatigue does not diminish
its emotions and desire.[2] It is the whole man ("l'espace entier")
which needs to be nourished and tended: "Cherchant, cherchant et
cherchant, c'est dans tout indifféremment que j'ai chance de trouver ce que je cherche puisque ce que je cherche je ne le sais"
("Seeking, seeking and seeking, in all things indiscriminately, I
might just find what I am seeking since I don't know what I am
seeking," *QJF,* p. 37). The very act of adventure with no particular
goal in sight except the experience of the whole is Michaux's artistic
continuum.

"Villes mouvantes" ("Mobile Cities") and "Adieu à une ville et
à une femme" ("Farewell to a City and to a Woman") reflect the
two kinds of travel that Michaux undertakes in his adventure:
travel in the physical world of outer space and travel into the imagi-

nary countries of inner space; for, in "Adieu à une ville et à une femme," he creates his first fictional place, Purkey. "Prédication" ("Sermon") and "Principes d'enfant" ("A Child's Principles") are groups of aphorisms, a form which appears from time to time throughout Michaux's work. In the first set, he states that people are not born aware of the world or of themselves; yet the world is so small (and by world here he means that experience is so limited) that something else is needed, even force, in order to create: "On . . . a terriblement besoin d'ailleurs" ("We . . . have a terrible need for elsewhere," *QJF,* p. 49). A possible response to this need is found in the second set of aphorisms in which the directness of the child's world view eliminates imposed facts: "Les clowns n'ont pas de père; aucun clown n'a de père; cela ne serait pas possible" ("Clowns do not have fathers; no clown has a father; that would not be possible," *QJF,* p. 51). The logic of the imagination gives new value to the experience.

Finding a rationale of pleasure in the terrain of the imagination which enhances outer space experiences is crystallized in "L'Epoque des Illuminés" ("The Era of Illuminati"). The illuminated ones are those who are bound by forms and imposed ideas. Their self-satisfied use of accepted techniques results in sterile, repetitious acts and actions. On the opposite side are those who are never complacent, but rely instead on instinct and natural forces in order to react and act; this group rejects conformity and defies the established order of things at every turn: "Il faudra être équipé à la minute" ("We will have to be ready at a moment's notice," *QJF,* p. 57). Hence, the future is accessible only to those who defy the form of order: "L'époque ne sera pas aux voyeurs, plutôt aux accélérés, aux sans famille, à ceux qui n'auront aucune technique, mais un imperturbable appétit" ("The era will not belong to seers, rather to the forgers, to those without ties, to those devoid of all technique, but with an imperturbable appetite," *QJF,* p. 59).

Appetite (desire, instinct, emotion) is demonstrated throughout the fifteen poems of the ninth section, "Poèmes," and accompanying the expression of the force of appetite is an attack on form as paralysis. In contrast with the narrative style of the preceding sections of the volume, the poems make no attempt to explain or explore inner conflicts; they are disputes which attest to inner disengagement: "Il ne s'agit pas ni d'être ni de ne pas être / il s'agit du *de ce que*" ("It is neither a question of being nor of not being / it is a matter of *the what,"* *QJF,* p. 63). Puns, surprise verbal pairings, nonsense terms, and other manifestations of word aggressiveness and deformations translate Michaux's struggle to break with form: "Je me blague / je me déruse" ("I kid myself / I outsmart myself," *QJF,* p. 78). Verbal humor and its acrobatic byplay accuse even the paper of victimizing the writer. In "Glu et gli,"[3] Michaux accuses the medium of paper of being so in love with ink that it remains external and incapable of depth; the very flatness of paper causes it to translate only the outer shell of an inner desire. Man needs new alphabets for such transcriptions. In the text, "Haine" ("Hatred"), he postulates the need for verbal exercise which would give color — intensity — to words, an experiment carried out in "Le Grand Combat," which contains Michaux's first use of magic ("Abrah! Abrah! Abrah!" *QJF,* p. 74) in an aggressive movement toward the discovery of the secret of life.

The attitude of combat which characterizes most of the poems extends the defiance of "L'Epoque des Illuminés" to the need for affirming the interior. In the only prose poem in the group, "Examinateur — Midi — " ("Examiner — Noon — "), Michaux combines defiance with desire and the problem of uncertainty. Yet, in a fascinating reversal of Valéry's evocation of high noon as fixity, Michaux portrays the examiner as limited to external conventionality, while the interior is the fixed point around which all else revolves and the point to which the adventurer wishes to journey. Bold self-seeking demands destruction of the trappings of form, including language. Like the rolling pebble in the text, "Caillou courrant," man in motion runs the risk of fragmentation in his need for confirmation, but fracture is preferred to the benediction of repetitious reasonlessness.

Of especial interest in the poems of *Qui je fus* is Michaux's continued refusal to engage in anecdote. Anecdote implies agreement, decoration, submission, and habit; it is serious, devoid even of the emotion of dispute. Emotion is clearly Michaux's chosen terrain. To this end, spoofing, satire, words of motion and change, imaginary people and places, fantasy, whimsy, and other active modalities alter exterior signs which are easily recognized and accepted by the intellect in an effort to free the internal reaction.

The concluding part of *Qui je fus* is significantly entitled "Fils de morne" ("Gloomy Sons"), and in a phrase it sums up the break with the dismal unchanged past. Man has lost his expression; he has suppressed his emotions to the point that he is devoid of feeling; he no longer becomes angry but remains so burdened by the malady of civilization (*morne*) that he practices calm and self-control, all the while taking precaution against disruptive emotions. Moreover, there are no remedies to his amortized existence. Science, industry, religion do not offer cures, but reinforce the need for precautions. Man is detached from his emotion which has become so interiorized and so rarely exteriorized that, unlike a dog which wags its tail and licks, nothing distinguishes him. Objective occupations and preoccupations have condemned man to a gloomy existence. This subdued, serious heritage of form is what Michaux rejects in *Qui je fus,* as he accepts the terrain of emotion and emergence. To externalize what has been interiorized is to deny the materialist-redemptorist-skeptic "qui je fus" composite which posits descriptive and prescriptive art and to embrace the seeker who follows his desires and responds emotively and immediately to the space around him.

II   *The Hospitality of Ecuador*

Michaux's first directed response to the world around him is found in the travelogue, *Ecuador* (1929). In keeping with the discoveries of *Qui je fus, Ecuador* consists of a rather faithful rendering of his trip to Ecuador with the poet Alfredo Gangotena and his year in Quito. Yet *Ecuador* contains little information and few details that pertain to Ecuador and Michaux's actual trip; for, while he actually visited the places mentioned, the journey and its journal are artistic pretexts for the discovery of self-value.

Ecuador is basically structured around a balance between inner reactions to outer stimuli, on the one hand, and external responses to inner sensations, on the other. The first-person narrator takes care to present a rather objective point of view which is, paradoxically, all the more subjective because of its selected range of material: "Vers trente ans, les études faites, c'est permis, on peut redevenir simple, et faire ainsi des découvertes" ("Around the age of 30, with studies out of the way, it is okay, one can go back to being natural, and thus make discoveries," *E,* p. 74).

In fact, selectivity characterizes all of *Ecuador*; there are diary entries which cover certain days literally from hour to hour and capture the immediacy and authenticity of a given experience. Other notations are summaries written so much later than the event described that the diarist cannot remember the date. And there are long lapses of time, as much as a month, with no explanations for the omissions. In addition to the obvious objectivity — which determined what was included for publication — there is also evidence of selectivity in the use of the Spanish language for the title, *Ecuador*. Throughout, Michaux uses the primary French term, *L'Equateur,* while the Spanish term *Ecuador* never appears in the volume. Moreover, the journey was not limited to Ecuador; Ecuador was the pivot point, the country to which the trip had been planned and undertaken. But some of the more unusual experiences took place in Peru and Brazil, where Michaux set out by horseback and canoe to travel the Napo and Amazon rivers. The misleading title affirms a certain personal and artistic ambiguity in the South American adventure, for in the opening preface Michaux admits that "au moment de signer, tout à coup pris de peur, il se jette la première pierre" ("at the moment of signing, suddenly overcome with fear, he casts the first stone at himself"). At the end of a second preface, he expresses amazement that a whole year of his life could be reduced to a few pages. What he ostensibly set out to do — to complete the break with his past formation and to adopt the terrain of creativity announced in *Qui je fus* — remains on one level incomplete: "Le voilà qui cherche. Mais il ne rencontre que brouillards. Alors, pour masquer son embarras, il prend une voix de pédagogue" ("There he is seeking. But he encounters only mists. So, in order to hide his embarrassment, he adopts a teacher's voice," *E,* p. 173). After all, nothing new was discovered in Ecuador ("Il n'a donc pas changé" — "He obviously has not changed," *E,* p. 172), but, on another level, Michaux had now affirmed through personal and artistic experiences the elected terrain of emotion: "Ce voyage . . . était plus fort que moi; comme une dette envers mon enfance, je me comprehends. / C'était agréable de songer que je pouvais faire ça, / Plus connue comme une vieille peau de révolte et de rage" ("That trip . . . I couldn't help it; like a debt to my childhood, I understand myself. / It was pleasant to think that I could do that / Better known as an old hide of revolt and rage," *E,* p. 171). The trip to Ecuador represented, then, Michaux's first concretion of desire, as inner space became externalized through the journal.

Michaux's election of the journal form to concretize what affects his emotions reinforces his earlier fascination with literature as deformation: "J'aime faire, créer . . . . Attaquer des objets, les modifier, les détruire, les refaire, les déplacer" ("I like to do, to create . . . . To attack objects, modify them, destroy them, redo them, displace them," *E*, p. 84). Traditionally, a journal is an accounting of events narrated in the first person by one who is both participant and witness, but, in Michaux's hands, it is not a means to set down experiences which one wishes to capture intact and preserve in a formal sense. Rather, Michaux's journal is a projection of the self beyond the outer surface of profiling the past. It is not the journey to Ecuador and the experiences encountered that are important. On the contrary, the trip and its resulting journal are indicators of the value of what one possesses: "or tout ce que vous possédez a une valeur de bonheur. Il suffit de trouver . . . l'être qui l'y trouve. Amasser des spectacles de bonheur. Devenir une usine à bonheur" ("Everything you possess obviously has a value of happiness. One need only find the being who finds it. Collect spectacles of happiness. Become a factory of happiness," *E*, p. 186). While Michaux does not confuse happiness with goodness (*bonté*), he does stress the verb *to give (donner)* as exchange throughout the final pages, entitled "Hospitalité." Exchange is not reciprocal giving and receiving, however, but the substitution of one thing for another, a way of disposing of one thing for another. Hence, the trip to Ecuador did not result in change and the journal did not record a give and take of experiences. Rather, Ecuador became the terrain of the discovery of exchange: the emotion of rage (revolt against the intellectual past) was replaced by the emotion of pleasure. The revelation of inner strength and possibilities became the freedom of self-knowledge: "L'enfant a besoin de savoir . . . c'est ce qui lui convient *à lui*; . . . Ainsi pour ce voyage . . . . Mais maintenant je sais ce qui me convient" ("The child needs to know . . . it is what suits *him*; . . . And so it is with this trip . . . . But now I know what suits me," *E*, p. 164).

Just as the exchange of emotions internally structures *Ecuador*, an exchange of style distinguishes it as well. Superficially, *Ecuador* is written in the notation form of diary entries; yet, consistent with the substitution of one emotion for another, Michaux would replace fragments which related an episode or described an event with poems. There are 22 formal free verse poems in *Ecuador*; some of these have titles ("Je suis né trouvé" — "I Was Born Found," and "Mort d'un cheval" — "Death of a Horse"), and, like proper diary entries, are situated geographically and temporally, such as "Arrivée à Quito" ("Arrival in Quito"), which is identified "à Quito, le 28 janvier" (*E*, p. 32). In addition to these poems, which are also printed in a different type from the prose diary entries, there are several notations (such as "La Crise de la dimension" — "The Crisis of Dimension") which could well be viewed as prose poems and some scenes are recounted in dialogue.

Documentation by hour and by day of the week is used more frequently than documentation by actual date. The presentness of the experience is thus reinforced by the absence of actual dating as well as by the dominance of the present tense. Effacement of the concrete details of the itinerary is further maintained, albeit paradoxically, by Michaux's attention to details. Early in the journal, he declares, "Un nom est un objet à détacher" ("A name is something to be undone," *E*, p. 29). Accordingly, the rain forest is mentioned only in passing, while one tree is evoked for its majesty; attention is drawn to *boa* as being masculine in French but feminine in Spanish; orchids are viewed as parasites; the tiger is no more than a jaguar; an island is dangerous to a ship. These kinds of details of deformation create "le gong fidèle du mot" ("The faithful gong of the word," *E*, p. 47) and are the environment which moves the observer-participant to respond. In contrast, the long trip by canoe down the Amazon results in unfamiliarity with the Amazon because its whole cannot be detached emotively: "Mais où est donc l'Amazone? . . . Il faut l'avion. Je n'ai donc pas vu l'Amazone. Je n'en parlerai donc pas" ("But then where is the Amazon? . . . I need a plane. I obviously haven't seen the Amazon. So I won't speak about it," *E*, p. 169). To see is to feel, to know is to experience, to understand is to be aware of value to the self and only to the self. The various styles of the journal reflect what is felt rather than note what is observed.

Ecuador ends with five prose sketches which do not seem to belong to it. Michaux describes them as memories which are pedagogical in tone; however, their content is related to the trip to Ecuador and they are certainly marked by personal experience. Yet each recollection is closer in style to Michaux's later excursions to imaginary countries than they are to the diary notations of *Ecuador*; and, like the experiences in *Ailleurs (Elsewhere)*, these vignettes are not limited to the form of a given trip — they are prose drawings which verbally simulate and synthesize inner reactions to outer events. Whereas the journal itself is written in fragments, the five verbal sketches at the end attach the parts of the diary (prose, poetry, dialogue) and make them cohere into the discovery which *Ecuador* confirms: the value of outer space depends on the possessions of inner space.

III *Inner Possessions*

Because *Qui je fus* is a work of separation from the past self, a self whose value was imposed by people, places, and things external to it, and because *Ecuador* in turn crystallizes projection towards an immediate future (who-I-can-be) through its suggestion of inner value, *Mes Propriétés (My Properties,* 1929)[4] must be seen as a work of inventory: who-I-am. The possessive *mes* of the title emphasizes the offensive thrust of this work in contrast with the defensiveness of *Qui je fus* and, to a great extent, *Ecuador*. Although fundamental differences such as the stylistic change from defense to offense and the move from exterior observation to inner examination tend to distinguish *Mes Propriétés*, there are equally valid internal reasons which make this work a companion piece to *Qui je fus* and *Ecuador*.

In the first place, the date of composition of *Mes Propriétés* places it close to the experiences in *Ecuador*. Some of the pieces were obviously composed before Michaux went to Quito ("Amours" — "Loves"); others, written concomitantly and published in 1928 while Michaux was in South America, relate to his heart condition which was magnified during the trip (for example, the five texts of "Luttes et mort" — "Struggles and Death"); still others post-date the trip ("Encore des changements" — "More Changes"). Second, there are major lexical items which internally link *Mes Propriétés* to previous words: *gong* as verbal force, interest in the roundness of the earth as actual flatness, a redefinition of spectacle, mixing of languages (French, English, Spanish), distortion of the whole through attention to details, literature as deformation. Third, the work is composed in fragments. Just as the entries of *Ecuador* are not written with a unified work in mind, but as the self is touched, *Mes Propriétés* consists of texts written without prior order in theme and style: "Ni thèmes, ni développements, ni construction, ni méthode . . . Les morceaux, sans liens préconçus, y furent faits paresseusement au jour le jour, suivant mes besoins"

("Neither themes, nor developments, nor construction, nor method . . . The items, without preconceived links, were done leisurely from day to day, according to my needs," *NR,* p. 204).

As *Ecuador* is described by Michaux as narcissistic ("J'ai fait à ma façon mon Narcisse" — "I did my Narcissus my own way," *E,* p. 171), so *Mes Propriétés* can be viewed as a self-centered work. However, Michaux adds to the egoism of *Mes Propriétés* a social dimension which is not present in his earlier works: "Ce livre, cette expérience donc qui semble toute venue de l'égoïsme, j'irais bien jusqu'à dire qu'elle est sociale . . . Ces imaginatifs souffrants, involontaires, perpétuels, je voudrais de cette façon au moins leur avoir été utile" ("This book, this very experience which seems totally based on egoism, I would go so far as to say that it is social . . . Those suffering, involuntary, perpetual dreamers, I would hope at least to have been helpful to them in this manner," *NR,* p. 205). The addition of a practical aspect to *Mes Propriétés* is not really a new attitude or desire on Michaux's part, for it does appear throughout *Les Rêves et la jambe*; but with *Mes Propriétés* he brings together in a single work all the experiences of exploration of inner and outer space which mark his previous writings and formulates the artistic base toward which the rest of his work will gravitate: "Sur un terrain on peut bâtir, et je bâtirai. Maintenant j'en suis sûr. Je suis sauvé. J'ai une base" ("On a terrain one can build, and I shall build. Now I am sure of it. I am saved. I have a base," *NR,* p. 125). Michaux's base is the projection of the imagination of inner space onto physical outer space: "la seule imagination de l'impuissance à se conformer" ("the only creative process was my inability to conform," *NR*, p. 204).

While the passages which make up *Mes Propriétés* were composed in a random manner, there is no mistaking the final deliberate order of the published whole. In fact, the definitive editions of 1935 and 1967 omit fifteen texts, including two whole sections (*Entre les lignes — Between the Lines* and *A Rotten Life*[5]), and rearrange the order of the three remaining sections: *Une Vie de chien (A Dog's Life),* which consists of twenty-eight prose musings; the ten prose observations of *Sciences naturelles,* which was moved from third position to second or middle; twenty-one free verse texts in *Poèmes*, which formed the second of the five original parts. Michaux's final arrangement of *Mes Propriétés* reveals the outlines of his elected creative terrain.

In *Une Vie de chien,* the key word is *soulagement* (relief, comfort), for the miserable life evoked by the title is countered by internal revolt which expresses the self. Words have therapeutic value and build up confidence ("Un Chiffon" — "A Scrap"), eliminate the superficial and artificial ("La Simplicité"), liberate the core of the self from the external problem of health and protection ("La Paresse" — "Laziness," "Bonheur" — "Happiness," "Le Honteux interne" — "The Shameful Interior"). Giving vent to emotions, especially anger ("Colère") is satisfying and eases, if only temporarily, the suffering of existence. In "Mes Occupations," Michaux fully embraces an attitude of offensive action through the verb *battre (to beat).* Man is vulnerable to outside pressures, demands, tensions, and, consequently, is ill; the corporeal limits inflict suffering, and there is no way to obtain a cure. As in "Fils de morne" (*Qui je fus*), all attempts at self-preservation create a hard shell which offers refuge from persecution inflicted from without ("Bétonné" — "Cemented In"). Health demands pride of self rather than shame of self. Letting inner psychological pressures out converts the potential of action into the actual wealth of being.

In "Mes Occupations," the immediate scene is a restaurant; one diner takes a dislike to another; instead of letting his hatred build and struggling to control it, he imagines fighting with the other and tearing him apart; at the end, he pays his bill and leaves. Nothing actually happens which alters the outer situation of a restaurant and its diners, but the diner who expresses himself through his imagination feels better. A certain temporary relief is experienced through verbal attack within.

In "Mes Propriétés," the longest text and the one from which the volume takes its name, all such feelings of hostility, terror, hate, derision, violence, suffering, fear, and horror are listed among the particular assets which the self possesses and can use to confirm its identity: "Je suis condamné à vivre dans mes propriétés et il faut bien que j'en fasse quelque chose" ("I am condemned to live on my properties and I must do something with them," *NR,* p. 120). The conversion of potential inner resources into actual assets which will be externally effective and operative is captured by the text "Projection." Use of the imagination improves the real, for it creates a "spectacle venu de moi" ("spectacle derived from me," *NR,* p. 147). Spectacle is not rejected by Michaux as is all too commonly assumed. Rather, external sights, as seen in their picturesque or

dull phenomenological existence, are dismissed; for Michaux refuses to confront the physical world, avoiding it by disengaging
himself from participation in his surroundings. Hence, in *Ecuador*,
he does not describe people, places, and things as they are in and of
themselves, but as he responds to them. An external spectacle has
value only to the extent that it affects the spectator; consequently,
the spectator's emotive reaction determines the experiences recounted in *Ecuador*, while, in *Mes Propriétés*, the kinds of responses that distinguish an individual are explored and projected
outward through intervention.

"Intervention" is the last text in *Une Vie de chien* and serves as
the counter-text to the opening misery expressed in the first one. Intervention is the method which closes the distance between the external real and the internal imagination, and it is an attitude of offensive action; "Autrefois, j'avais trop le respect de la nature. Je
me mettais devant les choses et les paysages et je les laissais faire. /
Fini, maintenant *j'interviendrai*" ("Formerly, I respected nature
too much. I placed myself before things and landscapes and I left it
to them. / No more, now *I shall intervene*," *NR,* p. 149). The
change from "let it happen" which is outer spectacle and defensive
in attitude to intervention as "making it happen," which is internal
and offensive, is the rejection of confrontation and the adoption of
substitution. The event or spectacle is neither prevented nor altered, but it is modified through the election of mutation.

By choosing the moment to intervene, there is a shift in the impact of the suffering caused by a given event; the suffering may remain, but it becomes the sufferer's choice as to when it occurs,
rather than his passive submission to the event. In such anticipation
of the event, Michaux reverses the order of affectivity and posits ef-
fectivity in its place. Being effective by intervening results in a kind
of comfort, strength, and remedy for the misery of life: "Quand
vous avez mal, il y a la souffrance du mal, il y a aussi le déséqui-
libre. Trouvez donc un deuxième, un qui s'y oppose" ("When you
hurt, there is the endurance of the hurt, there is also disequilibrium.
So find a second, one which is opposed to it," *P,* p. 153). As announced in the opening text of *Mes Propriétés*, intervention displaces weakness in order to establish stability; the power to recover
through the neutralization of opposing forces and tensions demands in turn a style of deformation; "Je ne laisse pas un mot dans
son sens ni même dans sa forme . . . Je pensais . . . que quand

j'aurais tout détruit, j'aurais de l'équilibre. Possible. Mais cela tarde" ("I don't leave a word in its meaning nor even in its form . . . I thought . . . that when everything was destroyed, I would have equilibrium. Perhaps. But it's taking a long time," *NR*, pp. 101-102). Realization of the effectiveness of disengagement replaces the disenchantment of confrontation.

Hence, the first section of *Mes Propriétés* is a carefully structured work which proposes aggression as a remedy for disorientation. The act of writing is no longer the stifling repetition of knowledge, but an act which generates knowledge. Description is abandoned for proscription; reflection is replaced by projection; submission is negated by election; the imagination affirms the reality of the self through intervention. As *Une Vie de chien* presents the project of intervention, the second section, *Sciences naturelles,* represents its possible application.

The power of the imagination can even be applied to the products of nature, especially the animal world which characterizes transformation. Just as the potential resources of the self are changed into actual possessions which modify the world, so do natural phenomena manifest changes in structure. The caterpillar becomes the butterfly through natural metamorphosis, and it is this kind of transmutation that Michaux applies to the elements which compose the world. In a sense, he transmogrifies. He deforms grotesquely and often humorously, but not so much for the purpose of entertainment as for evidence of man's creative power to improve the real, or, at least to improve his view of the real, and, consequently, to enhance his own position in the real. The creation of bizarre animals in "Notes de zoologie" — "La Parpue," "La Darlette," and "L'Emanglon"[6] — testifies to the inner freedom to intervene and generate spectacles rather than submitting to nature and being subjected to the humdrum sameness of its production (caterpillars always become butterflies, never elephants). These new observations renew the inner self by relieving both boredom and vulnerability. In "Notes de botanique," there are no leaves, and, in "La Race Urdes," Michaux creates his first anthropological people, who in this case are distinguished by their lack of need for women.

The ten texts of *Sciences naturelles* are written in the same style as the five recollections which close *Ecuador*, but they differ significantly in their use of the imagination. Where the five sketches at the end of *Ecuador* are based on factual observation of the unusual but no less authentic real world, the ten commentaries here destroy distance between the real and the fantastic; for the fantastic authenticates the real. There are trees and plants which do not have leaves, just as there are animals which, because of a given characteristic within a species, have different names. What Michaux does is to begin with the peculiarity, the deformation, and then to concentrate on its essence. Focusing on one detail generates an attitude of "why not," a sort of process of association which is not based on imposed definitions but on proposed applications. Hence, in the last text of this section, "Les Yeux" ("The Eyes"), there are big eyes, little eyes, aquatic eyes — eyes which express a quality, an attitude, a physical location, a personality, an emotion, an appetite, a desire; eye color and normal function are eliminated in favor of eyes as indicators of the possessions of inner terrain. Throwing all the eyes into a large cauldron at the end does not obliterate them, for the proprietor-poet can always bring them forth again, as he wishes. He is the master of the situation.

The usual connotation of the verb *to control* is "to hold things in check," but, for Michaux, it is "to use one's inner powers to modify external activities and events"; it does not mean to submit or repress, but to give free reign to one's emotions, feelings, reactions. One outlet near at hand is language. Language gives outer form to inner forces throughout the twenty-two free verse texts of *Poèmes*. As *Une Vie de chien* outlines the method of intervention and *Sciences naturelles* demonstrates examples of the kinds of interventions possible, *Poemes* captures the urgency of self-reliance and the immediacy of the relief through the release of inner needs. "Chaînes enchaînées" ("Enchained Chains"), for example, is based on word or vocal associations between *une (one)* and *hune (crow's nest)* and not on logical, much less pre-determined, associations. Sound is a chain which links disparates together and gives rise to new conjunctions and unities not possible in systematic terms. Meaning, then, is *gong*, the force of passion, not form. In "Je suis gong" ("I Am Gong"), gong is evoked as a subject-object based on the principles of energy. It represents the potential flow of creativity at the moment of impact; as a hard exterior, gong is the means for transmitting a message; its interior is the message itself. In this context, all of the *Poèmes* are gongs; touched by an event, the gong resounds, and its loudness, softness, highness, lowness depend on how it is touched. Originally, the term *poème* meant a work in verse, while *poésie* referred to anything which touched or moved a person. This original dictionary definition of poem and poetry accounts for Michaux's use of separate sections entitled "Poems" — gongs — in his early collected volumes.

"Compagnons," "Eux" ("Them"), "Articulations," "Rubili-lieuse,"[7] "Ra," "Rodrigue" are variations on the expression of inner possessions, forces. As Michaux states in the preface, these texts were invented "nerveusement et non constructivement selon ce que je pense du langage et des animaux" ("irritably and not constructively, according to what I think of language and animals," *NR*, p. 205). The linguistic inventions in *Poèmes* destroy fixed forms, words, and phrases by eliminating from them the weight of given responsibility and purpose. In "Amours," he reaffirms the role of seeker: "Cherchant je ne sais quoi de personnel / Je ne sais quoi à m'adjoindre dans cette infinie matière invisible et compacte" ("Seeking something personal / Something to make my own in this infinite, invisible, and compact matter," *NR*, pp. 184-185). The who-I-am, in exile from the Who-I-was and unable to know who-I-will-be, is in anguish over the nothingness that belongs to him in "Conseils" ("Advice") and "Emportez-moi" ("Take Me Away"), but his being gong at least affirms the potentiality of liberation of form in the future: "Oh! Espace! Espace non stratifié . . . Oh! Espace, Espace!" ("Oh! Space! Non-stratified Space . . . Oh! Space, Space!" *NR*, p. 200).

The call to space which ends *Mes Propriétés* is a projection of the self through verbal deformation into the indestructibility of non-form. Nothingness is the absence of stratification (definition), suffering, contradiction. Intervention into imposed hierarchical order, through verbal gonging from within to without, temporarily lifts him out of the present of structured complexity into the future of limitlessness. Utilization of his properties brings about freedom and gives value to the terrain of existence. The experience of non-stratification is salvation and hope.

CHAPTER 3

Plume and the Serenity of Night

L E noir est ma boule de cristal. Du noir seul, je vois de la vie sortir
(Black is my crystal ball. From black alone do I see life emerging, *P.*,
p. 85).

The composite emotional terrain of inner space which represents
man's proprietary assets — to do with as he pleases — provides the
base of offensive counteraction as the only means within human
grasp for the alleviation of the suffering experienced in contact
with outer space. Movement from within to without brings about a
measure of freedom from external causality; intervention through
the imagination disintegrates the oppressiveness of a situation and
dissolves its impact. But this manner of intervention remains volun-
tary, for it is undertaken with the acute awareness that there must
be discontinuity, even incoherence, in order for there to be relief
and salvation — however temporary. Rupture, for Michaux, is,
then, a willed deformation of the real through the freeing of inner
desires, appetites, instincts, emotions. Ever on the terrain of the affective self (of what touches one emotively), Michaux's work does
not explore the functioning of the imagination, but its effectiveness. The unfettering of the imagination by itself is not what frees;
rather it serves heuristically as an argument which postulates the
discovery of the purity of the self and its expression. The imagination is a guide to self-determination and self-approbation.

At night, imagination reaches its peak of activity, for the
prevailing diurnal order of limitation, confrontation, and dictation
disappears. Night agitates (*remue*); it is the time for offensive action, while day is accompanied by defensiveness. Hence, *night* is
the key word in Michaux's explorations of inner space between
1930 and 1935. Night affirms substance, as it obliterates form, localization, and spectacle.

In the 1945 and 1966 editions of his anthology *L'Espace du dedans* (*The Space Within*), Michaux destroys his first collective order and appears to return to his original compositional (volume by volume) order. Whereas *Un Certain Plume* (1930) precedes *Lointain intérieur* (*Far Away Inside*, 1938) and *La Nuit remue* (*Night on the Move*, 1935) precedes *Mes Propriétés* (1929), *Plume* is more related to *La Nuit remue* than to *Lointain intérieur*; and both works in turn spring from *Difficultés* (1930). Moreover, in *L'Espace du dedans*, *Difficultés* as well as *Le Drame des constructeurs* (*The Builders' Drama*, 1930) are merged with *Plume* and serve as transitional texts to *La Nuit remue*. In fact, only five of the texts listed as *Plume* texts in *L'Espace du dedans* are original to the 1930 *Un Certain Plume*.[1] Yet, regardless of order, there is no doubt that *Difficultés, Un Certain Plume,* and *Le Drame des constructeurs* belong together as interior movements and examples of intervention as the inner solution to the human condition, which is, in turn, summarized by the title, *La Nuit remue.*

I   *The Prose of Plume*

In the seven texts of *Difficultés*,[2] misfortune characterizes all human experience in outer space. These difficulties of suffering and deprivation are seemingly beyond solution; but, as the title implies, they can be overcome through the momentary, but rare, inner sensations of elevation which affirm the self. Throughout *Difficultés*, Michaux displays a rise and fall pattern which will recur in the rest of his work and which will all too frequently frustrate his reader. In "Chant de mort" ("Death Song"), for example, death is viewed as what terminates the life rhythm of elevation and defeat, yet there is supreme joy in this text, a joy which temporarily effaces all thought of death, finality, and loss. These moments of joy, however short-lived, make the hard base ("le sol dur") a valued possession: "Je retombai sur le sol dur de mon destin, destin à tout jamais le mien maintenant" ("I fell again on the hard ground of my fate, fate forever mine now," *PLI*, p. 128). To possess one's destiny is to have fortune, but to possess it demands also cognizance of the excruciating world which binds together human experience and destiny ("Destinée").

The opening text in *Difficultés* is "Portrait d'A" ("A's Portrait"), a highly autobiographical work which reflects on the impotence which occurs through education and exposure: Loss of perfection — man after the fall from grace — is described as comprehension of the dynamism and consequent multiplicity of the world. Born a "boule hermétique" ("hermetic sphere"), man learns from reading to distinguish between content and style, and from traveling that existence brings nothing but discomfort. The original sphere (unity) is literally cracked by life and loses its sense of indivisibility: "Il voudrait agir. Mais la boule veut la perfection, le cercle, le repos" ("He would like to act. But the sphere wants protection, the circle, rest," *PLI*, p. 117). Frustration between acting (confronting) and perfection is reaffirmed in "La Nuit des embarras" ("Night of Obstructions"), a text which deals with the nightmare of objects. Transformation through hallucinations and apparitions confirms the solitude of man's continual fall and increasing imperfectibility. Yet, unless there is fall — and night does repeat the fall — there can be no rise; without imperfection, there is no understanding of perfection. The nightmare of "La Nuit des embarras" is countered by "La Nuit des disparitions" ("Night of Disappearances") in which obscurity is a fortune, for the physical forms of the body and the world at large are not visible, and divisiveness and multiplicity cease.

The last text in *Difficultés* is significantly entitled "Mouvements de l'être intérieur" ("Movements of the Inner Being"). The inner terrain is evoked in terms of a powder keg, which upon explosion leads to knowledge of the immediate. Anger is at first juxtaposed with patience, yet both are inner reactions which in combination replace the sensation of weightiness with speed. When the natural velocity of emotions encounters the realm of virtues which outer space determines, the result can only be despair and defeat: "L'homme vaincu à l'avance" ("Man conquered in advance," *PLI*, p. 132). Life, as depicted even in the womb in the text "Naissance" ("Birth"), is a series of objects which represent human gestation. The character Pon[3] is born first from an endless series of forms (egg, fox, trombone) and finally from a woman. His birth into the heaviness of the world simulates both the loss of perfection of "Portrait d'A" and the debacle of experiences in "Mouvements de l'être intérieur."

Despite the rather pessimistic overtones of *Difficultés*, this group of seven texts represents the situation which is to be overcome through the use of inner forces and intervention. As weight characterizes this group, weightlessness is the salient feature of *Un Certain Plume*.[4] While *Difficultés* presents the problems to be solved and in no way expresses the impossibility of solution, *Un Certain Plume* explores the world as it might be if one had no inner possessions.

Plume is not a hero. Moreover, Plume is not really human, and his lack of a personality — his lack of properties — prohibits the possibility of a reader's identifying with him. Plume is unaware of the world around him; he does not complain, does not act, does not suffer, does not intervene. His lack of an inner terrain means that he is invulnerable to outer space; yet, at the same time, he is the constant dupe of outer space because he has no forces to release and can, therefore, never master, much less remedy, his situation. In fact, Michaux's sketches of Plume vary as to details (number of eyes, shape of head) because Plume has no temperament, no identity to be depicted. Plume's total inability to respond and react results in his constant role of victim: "Avec Plume, je commence à écrire en faisant autre chose que de décrire mon malaise. Un personnage me vient. Je m'amuse de mon mal sur lui" ("With Plume, I begin to write by doing something other than describing my uneasiness. A character comes to mind. I play with my ailment through him").[5]

Plume takes the knocks of existence because the blows do not affect him. Although the reader laughs at Plume, Plume is not even aware that he is an object of ridicule. But this laughter on the part of the reader represents the use of inner forces to remedy the external situation. Humor deforms the real and is directed outward; it provides temporary mastery over the situation. As the reader's laughter annihilates distance between the real (the reader's inner forces, terrain) and the imaginary (Plume), there is a moment of freedom and relief. In other words, Plume is not a literary convention but a stylistic intervention which, for a time, distracts the reader from his own difficulties and makes the world palatable. Plume does not react, but the reader does through laughter.

The publishing history of *Un Certain Plume* bears resemblance to Plume's own elasticity of form, and, on another level, it reveals Michaux's sustained interest in Plume as a demonstration of stylistic intervention. In the definitive version (1963), there are only thirteen prose narratives. But in the first 1930 printing there were five, which were later expanded into five parts and thirty-four chapters for another 1930 edition, which were then reduced to fourteen in 1938. Using the 1963 edition, tales one, two, three, four, and six date from the earliest publication of *Plume*; tales ten through fourteen were added in 1938; five, seven, and nine first appeared in the second 1930 publication. While chapter eight dates from 1930, it was originally part of the three nightmare scenarios, *Trois Nuits (Three Nights,* 1930)[6]; the original chapter ten, "On cherche querelle à Plume" ("Trying to Pick a Quarrel with Plume"), was not deleted until 1963.

The opening Plume text, "Un Homme paisible" ("A Peaceful Man"), was originally entitled "La Philosophie de Plume" ("Plume's Philosophy") and is, like the entire *Plume* collection, a work of inversion. *Peaceful* is used in a pejorative sense; because Plume neither resists nor offends, he is the butt of laughter. Like a feather, he is passive, weightless, and undirected. When his house is stolen, his wife slaughtered, and he is sentenced to be executed, he shows no emotions, but submits passively; in fact, he goes back to sleep. Life is disagreeable, Plume is agreeable; nonetheless, he is guilty. His very passivity and submissiveness bring about his defeat. While Plume is unaware of what has happened to him and is not affected by what will happen, he still remains the victim. In "Plume au restaurant" ("Plume at the Restaurant"), he is again victimized: he orders a cutlet which is not on the menu. Deviation from the normal brands him as a troublemaker and nearly lands him in jail. He remains a victim of fatigue which prevents him from sightseeing in "Plume voyage." The world continues as his implacable enemy throughout "Dans les appartements de la reine" ("In the Queen's Apartments"); while waiting for the king, the queen "seduces" Plume, who does as she tells him but never registers emotion or reflection at undressing and climbing into bed with her; ever the follower unable to think for himself, Plume is caught by the king.

Satire on how good life is for the living in "La Nuit des Bulgares" ("The Bulgarians' Night") finds Plume on a train with Pon, the character created in *Difficultés*. These two one-dimensional persons spend a nightmarish night throwing dead bodies off a train; at the first stop, they flee because they are unable to master the situation. Intervention is unknown to Plume. When he attempts to project his imagination and create a spectacle in "La Vision de Plume" ("Plume's Vision"), he conjures up a scene of action, which does not give him any escape. Significantly, "La Vision de

Plume" is one of the five original texts, but in later publications the epigraph is omitted. Michaux's original introduction stresses the necessity of night for those to whom day brings nothing[7]; yet Plume's vision does not bring him any relief in its gestation. Again, he is the passive spectator who is unmoved emotively and intellectually.

Plume as unmoved spectator appears in "Plume avait mal au doigt" ("Plume Had a Sore Finger"), although in this text alone Plume does assert himself to a degree. His sore finger is amputated by a surgeon against his futile arguments. Plume's wife chastizes him for letting it happen, but in a rare moment of disagreement and anger, he rebuffs her: "Ecoute . . . ne te tracasse pas pour l'avenir. J'ai encore neuf doigts et puis ton caractère peut changer" ("Listen, don't worry about the future. I still have nine fingers and then your personality can change," *PLI*, p. 161). Submission is typical of Plume, but rationalization is a rare process for him. In "Plume avait mal au doigt," he is not just the phlegmatic prey of external space; rather, he is the victim of his own inner space because of his attempt to confront the world on the basis of logic. Although confrontation fails (Plume's finger is amputated), his moment of anger does at least bring him a measure of release when dealing with his wife. Nonetheless, he remains untouched by the event, and he cares neither about his mutilation nor about his wife's feelings.

Originally entitled "La Nuit des assassinats" ("The Night of Assassinations") in *Trois Nuits,* the eighth Plume text, "L'Arrachage des têtes" ("The Taking-Off of Heads") is the only text in *Un Certain Plume* which does not mention Plume by name. Consciousness is equated with confrontation with outer space, while its effacement is synonomous with relief and suggests night as the time for escape: "Enfin ils se perdent dans la nuit, et ça leur est d'un grand soulagement; pour eux, pour leur conscience. Demain, ils repartiront . . . Ils essaieront de se faire une vie" ("They finally disappear into the night, and that is a great comfort to them; for them, for their consciences. Tomorrow, they will start up again . . . They will try to make a life for themselves," *PLI*, p. 165). But the futility of the effort to make a life through one's awareness is reinforced in "Une Mère de neuf enfants" ("A Mother of Nine Children"). Ironically, the mother is a Berlin prostitute who accosts Plume, and he submits to being raped without any emotion; the event will merely become a pleasant memory of his trip and nothing more.

The distractions of travel (external spectacle) continue to leave Plume unaffected in "Plume à Casablanca," a text added to the series in 1938. Plume's travel problems are the daily errands which must be done and his worry over customs. In "L'Hôte d'honneur du Bren Club" ("The Guest of Honor at the Bren[8] Club"), a text which was also added in 1938, Plume eats regardless of the situation: bad food, appearance of a snake, the baring of a woman's breast. In a moment of distraction in "Plume au plafond" ("Plume on the Ceiling"), another 1938 addition, Plume is caught on the ceiling and all rescue attempts fail: "Pas de choix dans le malheur, on vous offre ce qui reste" ("No choice in misfortune, you are offered what is left," *PLI*, p. 174). This line summarizes the *Plume* series of texts; no matter what happens, it is a misfortune. Even in the text which was deleted in 1963, "On cherche querelle à Plume" ("Trying to Pick a Quarrel with Plume"), Plume's anger confirms his bad luck. In his only demonstrative act of violence, a duel and the subsequent slaying of all the gentlemen at a party, Plume winds up first in the hospital before being sent to the war front; he pours iodine all over the nurse and leaves in a moment of triumph. In a sense, Plume as a soldier seems to succeed in overcoming the persecuters of outer space by releasing an inner emotional terrain of anger. But Plume's anger is not one of projection and actual intervention; while he changes the situation through confrontation, he never gains mastery over it. In addition, Plume's own attitude is consistent throughout the text; he does not feel relief, nor is he affected by the event. Plume has no properties; not even his anger belongs to him.

The final text finds Plume helping legless people in "Plume et les culs-de-jatte" ("Plume and the Legless Cripples"). The irony lies in Plume's apparent attempt to help others, but even this kind of action is a confrontation with outer space and it fails. Creation is not tender; responsibility for others does not bring inner relief. The only reaction Plume has while helping the legless cripples up a tree where they are having a reunion (a situation which further underscores the ridiculousness of outer space) is physical and psychological exhaustion: "Fatigue! Fatigue! On ne nous lâchera donc jamais?" ("Fatigue! Fatigue! Won't we ever be free?" *PLI*, p. 176).

Plume is caught in the absurdity of outer space and without the resources of inner space, without properties. Literally an object in a

Sartrian sense, Plume exists, but he is unaware that he exists. He is unmoved by events and people. In Michaux's universe, Plume has no properties and, consequently, he has no identity. Just as he is never the same in Michaux's sketches, throughout *Un Certain Plume* his nationality, profession, marital status, and interests vary from text to text. He cannot be described because he has no inner terrain, no base from which he can begin to operate in the external world. Plume is the hermetic sphere of *Difficultés*: perfect because he is unaware of the dynamism of the world. And Plume is like night: formless, weightless, and indivisible. In his very shapelessness, he gains a position of prominence in Michaux's work, for Plume personifies night in its effacement of confrontation, limitation, and multiplicity. While the reader remains unable to identify with Plume, the reader does enjoy him as a fictional character whose lack of comprehension and suffering concretize the might-have-been and might-be: freedom from external causality through the imagination.

Michaux's use of the imagination as a stylistic intervention which provides the reader with momentary relief from the outer world is maintained in *Le Drame des constructeurs (The Builders' Drama),* a one-act play written in 1930 and performed in 1937. The play concerns the inmates of an asylum who play at building things: dice, a city in a thumb, theaters with no public, a city in a stomach. Through their insane fancies, they actually succeed in making their situation acceptable. Among the characters are eight lunatics, evoked by a single letter each (A, B, C, D, E, F, G, H), the guards who are hostile, and God. God is against those who interfere with His creation; hence, He is kindly disposed towards the lunatics whose interventions are imaginary only and He is against the guards who oppose the imagination and whose interference causes suffering. Nothing changes, however, for the play ends as it begins, except for the reader-spectator who finds himself on the side of the lunatics as a moment of relief from the real. Michaux's change in the title from *fous (lunatics)* to *constructeurs (builders)* in 1963 emphasizes the affirmative and serious nature of this play, which at first glance seems a mere piece of whimsy. Similar to the absurdist plays of the 1950's, *Le Drame des constructeurs* offers laughter and the imagination as valid bulwarks against the absurdity of the human condition. As an anti-play, it rebounds on the viewer and makes him uncomfortable, as he supports fantasy (the lunatics) and turns against reality (the guards).[9]

II *The Poetry of Night*

Resistance through offensive inner action not only unifies Michaux's three 1930 works, *Difficultés, Un Certain Plume,* and *Le Drame des constructeurs,* but it also is the basic thematic and stylistic structure of *La Nuit remue (Night on the Move,* 1935). Divided into two parts, the first section consists of twenty-six prose recitations, while the second part consists of seven "formal" poems, five in free verse and two in prose. With *La Nuit remue,* Michaux's pattern of juxtaposing prose narratives with texts generically labeled "poems" is firmly established. Moreover, the section designated as "poems" is in quantitative terms smaller than the preceding prose renditions, while qualitatively the poems are summary capsules which contain the full impact of the potential suggested in the prose explorations. The prose texts pose various possibilities, while the poems demonstrate their realization. This distinction between formal prose and poetry continues to characterize Michaux's work. Night or potential — regardless of the written collection in question — stirs up poems. The unformed prose (unformed as unclassifiable except as opposed to a basic visual form called poetry) awakens the inner self and prepares the self for the onslaught of light. Poetry becomes the specific result of these inner activities, for it reacts against the mechanical, oppressive day. Prose, on the other hand, is nocturnal in its anticipation of means to counter the prevailing diurnal order, but poetry is what is agitated within at night in order to maintain the inner terrain of the self during the daytime of limitation, localization, and multiplicity.

Hence, the Michaux poem is a text of the inner self projected outward. It scorns and defies outer space, as it refuses to imitate the real and rejects all concepts of commitment to the real. Michaux's poetry is consistently identified by him as poetry. Consequently, the reader has no trouble recognizing stylistically and generically, even descriptively, the Michaux poem. The Michaux poem is diurnal; it has shape, prescribed limits, demonstrates awareness, and is multiple in that it is either in free verse (in the widest sense of the term) or in prose. On the other hand, Michaux's prose cannot be described; it is night, and, as night, it is formless because it assumes all forms and all potentiality of form.

In one sense, Michaux's separation of prose and poetry goes counter to contemporary writing which tends to fuse genres and which claims that all writing is a poetic, unformed compository and repository of the best of human creativity. Such a concept of the role of poetry in the modern world is, indeed, alien to Michaux's universe of inversion which repudiates confrontation with the real, but which at the same time finds no salvation in the imagination. If anything, Michaux is a poet-actor, never a poet-spectator, who uses the imagination as a means to discover the attitude of offensive action which makes diurnal (or real) existence bearable. He never pretends to ennoble or even better the human condition. His sole effort is directed towards resistance and self-protection. Only the unformed night or prose can arm man sufficiently to oppose the spectacle of day. Hence, there are no Plume poems, only Plume prose texts because Plume has no inner forces to agitate at night and to marshal against the coming of day. Plume, as his name implies, remains weightless; he never really exists because he has no inner terrain. On the other hand, *La Nuit remue* contains a section of poems which do intervene in the order of day and through intervention ease somewhat the oppressiveness of existence.

The twenty-six texts of *La Nuit remue* represent all possible forms of prose from simple narration and description to scientific criticism. The opening text, "La Nuit remue," continues the possessiveness of *Mes Propriétés*[10] by examining two resources: "ma chambre" ("my room") and "ma nuit" ("my night"). The bitter daily life ("l'amère vie quotidienne," *NR*, p. 10) is countered through projections of the imagination at night. Objects in the room are animated as the external, identifiable self merges with the gulf of night. At the end, he intervenes in his own fantasies in order to affirm his inner terrain.

The second text, "Mon Roi" ("My King"), presents action as a moral and creative force. The King is a master proprietor, literally absolute, who is always victorious in the on-going struggle, yet, he too is a possession, for he is consistently evoked as *my* King. In fact, the King cannot exist unless he has a subject who recognizes him as king. As a possession, the King suggests the original property of strength and action latent in man. The problem is to struggle against the subordination of the self to the King who is everywhere: in the privacy of the bedroom, on the side of adversaries in outer space, in control of all distractions, even in causing the loss of a fiancée. All homages to this king are in vain because his emotions are imperceptible. Nonetheless, through the continual revolt of the King's subject-victim (summarized in the constant use of the prefix *re-* which denotes recurring action), there is temporary release. It does not matter that the King is always victorious; what counts is the endless beginningness — possibilities — that struggle against the King represents. The King is a prized possession of inner space because the subject (and by extension the reader) can release hostility on him and thereby gain a moment of repose.

The value of inner activity and its subsequent release of energy can be found in all the texts of *La Nuit remue*. For example, in "Le Sportif au lit" ("The Sportsman in Bed"), closed eyes signify the time for action, the freeing of dreams, while in "En respirant" ("While Breathing"), the sound of hard breathing is presented as generative of the imagination and comfort. "La Nuit des noces" ("The Wedding Night") renounces release brought about by any act which causes harm to another; only one's own inner self, no matter how precarious and defenseless it may be, is valid, as Michaux summarizes in "Etapes" ("Stages"). Nature too serves as a stimulus which activates the imagination of inner self. In "Conseil au sujet des pins" ("Advice on the Subject of Pine Trees"), the breeze is found to be round and therefore evocative of dreaming. In "Conseil au sujet de la mer" ("Advice on the Subject of the Sea"), rugged waves during a storm can excite the imagination, while severe storms erase horizonality, limitation, and raise self-doubt: "Cette eau vous fait sentir en vous même l'absence d'une vraie base qui puisse servir en *tout* cas" ("This water makes you feel within yourself even the absence of a true base which might help *no matter* what happens," *NR*, p. 34).

The need to establish and recognize a true base is clearly presented in several texts (most notably "Dessins commentés — "Annotated Sketches"), which describe and interpret the significance of some pencil drawings made earlier. This text represents Michaux's earliest known example of writing on his own plastic art as a means to reveal the inner self countering the real. None of the sketches evoked can be said to be authentic reproductions of outer space: three multi-faced men, a lacy head, an octopus as a man, a horse in conversation with a stag which on closer examination is a doe, a princess whose hair is in the form of damsels. But each sketch is a form of intervention through the imagination.

Frustrations of diurnal existence are also found in "L'Auto de l'Avenue de l'Opéra" ("The Car of the Avenue of the Opera"), "Le Lac" ("The Lake"), "Bonheur bête" ("Stupid Happiness"), "Les Petits Soucis de chacun" ("Everyone's Little Cares"), "Déchéance" ("Downfall"), and "Emme et son parasite" ("Em and Her Parasite"). Juxtaposed to these texts are others which evoke the release from the oppressive real through the complete absence of encounter and confrontations. "Le Fort" ("The Strong Man") is so strong that he is not affected by life. The Giant Barabo and his brother Poumapi daily fight fiercely as a means of obliterating existence in "L'Age héroïque" ("The Heroic Age"). The two parts of "Vers la sérénité" ("Towards Serenity")[11] suggest an elected kingdom in which there are no regrets, only peace of mind.

The final text in the prose section of *La Nuit remue* represents Michaux's first detailed discussion of a drug experience in near-clinical terms: "L'Ether" ("Ether").[12] In the introduction, he observes that because man wants to get rid of his energy and personality, he constantly wants to be in a state of shipwreck: "[L'Homme] a besoin de faiblesse . . . D'une façon ou d'une autre, il lui faut être vaincu . . . il ne rêve que de dégringoler dans la faiblesse la plus entière" ("Man needs weakness . . . One way or another, he wants to be conquered . . . he dreams only of tumbling down into the most complete weakness," *NR*, p. 65). Man cannot gain serenity, the absence of encounter, as long as he is engaged in any sort of struggle. In this sense, the text "Mon Roi," for example, expresses man's need to be a subject, a victim, eternally vanquished. But, by expending his energy in a struggle with his King, the subject does gain momentary tranquillity although the King will return. The question that Michaux raises at the end of the prose texts of *La Nuit remue* is how to get rid of all energy and gain calm (". . . comment se défaire de ses forces et obtenir le calme," *NR,* p. 66). Ether as a form of drug taken is one means used, but it proves to be deceptive. In "L'Ether," Michaux discovers first the marvelous loss of any possession, complete freedom, but this loss also means the loss of identity. Even though the experience is an adventure in rapid thought, "une trémulation de l'esprit" ("a tremor of the mind," *NR*, p. 79), it remains worrisome because of its somersault effect and strange after-effect of loss of courage. While Michaux does seem to find value in ether as an opportunity for self-observation

— namely, separation of the diurnal self from the nocturnal one — and the experience of overcoming time, he does not find calm but increased energy, "une jouissance en cascade" ("a cascading joy," *NR*, p. 78). Just as the experience of opium in *Ecuador* was not successful in bringing relief, the experience of ether in *La Nuit remue* raises more problems than it solves; but Michaux does not close out the possibility of using artificial stimulants for the release of inner forces and the ultimate gain of inner peace.

While the prose texts of *La Nuit remue* explore various and widely differing means of intervention in the world through the imagination in an effort to repudiate the limitations of outer space, the seven poems which conclude the volume confirm the effectiveness of projecting the inner self. In "Contre!" ("Counter!"), the self is defended through the construction of interior barricades which prevent relationship with the world at large. The very title is in the imperative form of the verb of action, *contrer, to counter* or *go against*; moreover, it is in the familiar second person singular, which indicates evidence of its effect through personal experience. In addition to the command form, the future tense of hope through action appears throughout the text, as well as the fraternal *nous* (*we*). To be opposed to the real is to reject all acceptance and participation in the world. Here, as in the prose texts of the volume, inversion is the structuring principle. Defense becomes offense, as blackness becomes the positive mode of existence: "Dans le noir nous verrons clair mes frères. / Dans le labyrinthe nous trouverons la voie droite" ("In the dark we shall see clearly my brothers. / In the labyrinth we shall find the right path," *NR*, p. 84).

To counter is to remain in a state of constant action, which is exemplified in both "Nous autres" ("We") and "Comme je vous vois" ("As I See You"). There is neither triumph nor victory, for there is never arrival at a given destination; all is found in the struggle, and only death brings final release from the fight, which characterizes the series of complaints that constitute life ("Le Livre des réclamations" — "The Book of Claims"). Yet, because there are so many things lacking, man aspires to plenitude as in the poem "Ma Vie" ("My Life"): "A cause de ce manque, j'aspire à tant. / A tant de choses, à presque l'infini . . ." ("Because of this lack, I aspire to so much. / To so many things, almost to infinity. . . ," *NR*, p. 92). It is the imagination which acts as a force of self-identification; through it come reinforcement, disengagement from con-

frontation ("Tu t'en vas sans moi, ma vie" — "You are going away
without me, my life," *NR*, p. 92), and recognition of the need for
an absolute beyond the inner self, discoverable only on the ground
of inner terrain.

The hidden resources of inner terrain are evoked in the prose
poem, "Icebergs." While the greater part of an iceberg is unknown
and yet to be explored, it, nevertheless, represents unfettered soli-
tary freedom. Self-sufficient and uncontaminated, the iceberg is
not dependent on outer space for either its existence or its definition; the very fact that its greater part is a mystery to the world
without is a source of freedom and innocence. Described as cathe-
drals without religion ("cathédrales sans religion," *NR*, p. 93), yet
frozen in such a solid state as to defy any effort to touch their actual substance, icebergs testify to man's latent potential for self-ful-
fillment: "Icebergs, Icebergs, Solitaires sans besoins . . . Parents
des îles, parents des sources, comme je vous vois, comme vous
m'êtes familiers . . ." ("Icebergs, Icebergs, Hermits without need
. . . Parents of the islands, parents of the sources, how I see you,
how familiar you are to me . . . ," *NR*, p. 93).

The framework of detachment expressed in "Icebergs" also
structures the last text in *La Nuit remue*, "Vers la sérénité"
("Towards Serenity"). The goal of refusal is to attain freedom
from disruption and agitation: "Ainsi à l'écart, toujours seul au
rendez-vous, sans jamais retenir une main dans ses mains, il songe,
le hameçon au coeur, à la paix, à la damnée paix lancinante, la
sienne, et à la paix qu'on dit être par-dessus cette paix" ("Thus
apart always alone at the rendezvous, without ever keeping a hand
in his hands, he dreams, with a barb in his heart, of peace, of the
damned throbbing peace, his own, and of the peace said to be beyond that peace," *NR*, p. 95). The tranquillity desired is damned
because it can only be gained through the repudiation of all com-
promise; it throbs because it measures the pulse of inner terrain,
and its pulsation is evidence of the effort demanded. Disturbance
from the release of energy and personality eventually brings the
motionless calm sought, for the ultimate peace evoked is, of
course, death as the absence of struggle. The struggle is the refusal
to submit to being knocked about by life, and the greater the con-
sistency of the fight the nearer the attainment of peace. Hence, the
significance of the title is not found in the noun of place or destination, *sérénité*, but in the preposition of direction, *vers,* which emphasizes non-acceptance of the world as it is.

The seven poems which conclude *La Nuit remue* confirm Michaux's pattern of disengagement from outer space through the agitation of inner space as man's only means of self-realization. But it is interesting to note that only in the opening poem, "Contre!", is there any evidence of Michaux's adoption of an aggressive style. Even in the twenty-six prose texts which compose the first section of *La Nuit remue* there are few examples of language as a hostile weapon which expresses scorn and defiance. On the contrary, all the texts of *La Nuit remue,* including "Mon Roi" and "Contre!", are projections of intervention which detach the inner self from confrontation with the oppressive real; they are texts which lead towards serenity, as they release the poet and his reader from encounters with external spectacle. The formlessness of night stirs up the potential within to turn away from outer space and gain freedom from the frustrations of diurnal order. While unclouded calm may remain elusive in the permanent sense, the texts confirm the possibility of liberation from restraint and the experience of plenitude and serenity. Nocturnal activity so arouses man's latent but rich inner resources and provides outlets for his energy that the difficulties of the diurnal spectacle may be overcome. By projecting a Plume-like object to receive the blows of the oppressive real, the unity of thought and action is attained and known. In the manner of an iceberg, the labyrinth of man's inner terrain straightens and solidifies, as the drama of counteractive intervention builds self-confidence. Because night is deliverance from the prevailing outer order of limitation, it stirs up the possibility of adventuring further towards the serenity desired — and beyond.

CHAPTER 4

Eureka! Liberation of the Imagination

C'ÉTAIT à l'arrivée, entre centre et absence, à l'Euréka, dans le nid de bulles . . . (It was at the finish, between center and absence, at Eureka, in the nest of bubbles. . . , *PLI*, p. 38).

The Michaux adventure beyond the self represents the artistic discovery of the imagination and the personal triumph of loss of the painful self-centered world. Journeying into the imagination releases a new consciousness which permits, first, detachment from any relationship with the world and, second, brings into being images of what is not in outer space. Finding a terrain between one's center of identification through confrontation and one's absence of the experience of exile and fear which result from such confrontation — "entre centre et absence" — is realized by actualizing inner space which expresses the pure self: Eureka! Yet the voyage to such a non-personal world is possible only through total control; it is neither an escape from the world as a means of self-protection (or even self-delusion), nor a manifestation of belief in the imagination as evidence of a marvelousness latent in outer space. Michaux's Eureka does not deny the self; rather, it expresses liberation from suffering and alienation and the possibility of identification with others because of the discovery that this pure self does exist far away inside (*Lointain intérieur*), and, what is more, its reality can be demonstrated. As *Lointain intérieur* makes the thoughts and aspirations of inner space concrete, *Ailleurs (Elsewhere)* provides further testimony to the triumph of the discovery. The imagination defeats suffering by realizing inner freedom and projecting it outward.

I   *The Autonomy of Inner Space*

Properly speaking, the collected volume *Lointain intérieur (Far Away Inside,* 1938 and 1963) has six distinct parts: *Entre centre et absence (Between Center and Absence,* 1936), *La Ralentie (Woman in Slow Motion,* 1936), *Animaux fantastiques (Fantastic Animals), L'Insoumis (The Rebel), Je vous écris d'un pays lointain (I Am Writing to You from a Faraway Land,* 1937), and *Poèmes.* A cursory glance at the titles of the sub-sections shows concentration on more abstract and less physical activities. In fact, the titles indicate a remoteness from recognizable locations, actual time, and familiar points of view. Separation from the known establishes temporal and spatial distances, as Michaux moves to a point within, which may even seem artistically inaccessible in its foreignness. Yet, the general title for the collection of these six parts represents such a linguistic contradiction that problems of definition in terms of outer space associations cease.

The very grammatical ambiguity of *Lointain intérieur* as a title so defies reader confrontation that it is accepted "as is" without further attempt to impose outer qualification and clarification upon its actual meaning. *Lointain intérieur* is not actual as a location, much less as a linguistic locution. The two terms which compose the title can be read as two nouns, two adjectives, or any of two combinations of adjectives and nouns. In addition, each of the two terms has precise connotations which Michaux nullifies by placing them together in such a way that the integrity of each term is lost. *Lointain* as a noun means either distance, usually a remote place, or background; in adjectival usage, it denotes *far* in terms of either time or space. By contrast, *intérieur* as a noun refers to that which is within, to the central part of something, to a private house or home, to one's country, or even, upon occasion, to a person who does not like to go outside; as an adjective, *intérieur* means *internal,* but it is even more restricted than that inasmuch as it relates to non-physical matters and contrasts with external limits. Moreover, *intérieur* is a less intimate term than *inner* or *inward,* and it tends to be more abstract as well. While *lointain* suggests the removal of connections, *intérieur* indicates connections for the purpose of contrast; and, while *lointain* demands separation even to the point of inaccessibility, *intérieur* insists on belonging to something as either its reverse or its core for definition. By using *lointain* and *intérieur* together, with no indication as to their referentials, Michaux destroys their actuality of definition in terms of outer space and creates a new autonomy of their authenticity in terms of inner space.

Hence, *Lointain intérieur*, as a title, emphasizes the power of the imagination to create through the dispersal of what is and the presentation of what is not. By moving far away inside, Michaux projects the self and the text as expression of the self beyond all limitation, even that of language: "Il n'est pas un moi. *Il n'est pas dix moi. Il n'est pas de moi. MOI n'est qu'une position d'équilibre.* (Une entre mille autres continuellement possibles et toujours prêtes.) Une moyenne de 'moi', un mouvement de foule. Au nom de beaucoup je signe ce livre" ("There isn't one me. *There aren't ten me's. There is no me. ME is only a position of equilibrium.* [One among a thousand others which are continually possible and always ready.] An average of "me", a crowd movement. In the name of many I sign this book," *PLI*, p. 217).

The peripheral inversion which the title *Lointain intérieur* evokes is announced in *Entre centre et absence,* first published as a separate work in 1936. Again, a seeming contradiction of terms characterizes the title. The problem of being between two opposing states of existence (center as the fixed immobile self and absence as the dynamic mobile self) is not one of conflict between a definite position (center) and an indefinite one (absence), for the title affirms neither position. In fact, the title does not refer to position at all, but to a point of equilibrium between two possible positions. To leave one's center — one's fixed, formed identity — and to move towards, but never to, freedom from the limits which give form to that personality is a Eureka which defeats the suffering of self yet does not deny awareness of the triumph over that suffering. The potential of reshaping the self through the freedom of participation (possible because one is no longer irrevocably at center) is known through the images projected — images which have no direct relation to the actuality of self, but, at the same time, images which maintain an awareness of that actuality. The fine line lies in the role which Michaux assigns to consciousness; he does not release the subconscious; on the contrary, he releases the self-conscious in order to capture the pure conscious or pure self which is unfettered by the actuality of anguish. He becomes detached from the personal position of participation, as he becomes objective in a non-personal (but never impersonal) transcription of discovery of the pure self. While liberation through the imagination does not redeem or even conquer the painful self of actuality, it displaces the fact of suffering through a counterbalance of non-suffering; the momentary result is a neither-nor evocation, an equilibrium which neutralizes two opposing forces through resistance to both.

In the text of the same title as the volume, "Entre centre et absence," Michaux celebrates the loss of both physical suffering and psychological anguish. Convalescing from a long illness and being in a more weakened (exposed) state than usual, the patient projects inner desires outward: "Je passe . . . Inouïe simplicité! Comment ne t'avais-je pas devinée? . . . Sans ruse, le poulet sort parfait d'un oeuf anodin . . ." ("I pass . . . Unheard-of simplicity! How could I not have figured you out? . . . Without trickery, the chick is born perfect from an anodyne egg . . .," *PLI*, pp. 37-38). Release of a fully developed image (chick) is attained, first, through the desire to break out from the actual condition and, second, from the projection of the opposite condition. The vivid presence of what is not physically in the room confirms the image-making power, a new property which verifies the imagination through the actual seeing, and seeing clearly, what is beyond the power of the mind to grasp: "C'était pendant l'épaississement du Grand Ecran. Je VOYAIS! Se peut-il, me disais-je, se peut-il vraiment ainsi qu'on se survole?" ("It was during the thickening of the Big Screen. I COULD SEE! Is it possible, I said to myself, is it really possible to fly over oneself?" *PLI*, p. 38).

The product of the power to create images is brought about through control over the center of the self and a freeing of that immobile self (reinforced by the fact that the actor-spectator is confined to bed) beyond the self into a level of participation which has no tie with reality: "C'était à l'arrivée, entre centre et absence, à l'Euréka, dans le nid de bulles. . . ." The ellipsis at the end of this text indicates a continuing of the displacement of the self through the imagination. While Michaux never implies that what is seen is true or of any value, the reader, through the final suspension points, is left with his own screen and with the possibility of his own discoveries. The ellipsis suggests strongly that the solitude of the self can be overcome for him as it is for the fictive persona of the text and that a new relationship with the world can be established.

Since the first publication of *Lointain intérieur* in 1938, the text "Entre centre et absence" has been placed at the end of the *Entre centre et absence* section, where it serves as a résumé of the work as testimony ("JE VOYAIS") to the image-making power within and as an introduction (the ellipsis) to the rest of the collected volume. Yet, in 1936, this text was the opening one[1] of *Entre centre et absence*: concentration ("je passerai," "je passe") can alter the situation if not the event and all that follow are products of the imagination as seen on the screen of artistic intervention.

Intervention as a means of displacing the suffering of actuality through the power of the imagination is clearly presented in the five parts of "Magie" ("Magic"), which serve as an introduction to the problem and to the denial of the very problem posed. The first one outlines futile attempts to fuse the self with other objects: an apple, the Escaut river, another apple: "*Souffrir* est le mot" ("*Suffer* is the word," *PLI*, p. 10). Loss of self (center) demands the patience and courage to endure what is injurious and painful; the effort to sustain what is imposed by the mind must be endured to such an extent that upon arrival in the apple, the poet is frozen, immobile. But, the ability to seduce and, consequently, to change the self is, in the second part, evidence of possession of the self because one can leave and return at will. Isolating the center ("boule") in "III," he studies it and finds that detachment offers a form of immunity from reaction to stimuli and temporarily buries anguish. Isolation of an instance of suffering is the subject of "IV," in which the sufferer concentrates on a toothache and on an earache in order to overcome them. Once the actual pain is detached from the rest, it ceases to exist, for its equilibrium has been changed.

The capacity to define the self and then to deny the discovery entails the discipline of vigilance, which prevents Michaux from accepting the coincidence of the imagination and the real; the two must remain disparate, for only the imagination triumphs over the real and fortifies its proprietor with enough freedom and power of freedom to defy the actual event by changing the situation: "Grâce à cette discipline, j'ai maintenant des chances de plus en plus grandes de ne jamais coïncider avec quelqu'esprit que ce soit et de pouvoir circuler librement en ce monde" ("Thanks to this discipline, I now have an increasingly greater chance of never being in agreement with any spirit and of being able to move about freely in this world," *PLI*, p. 14). Hence, Michaux's use of the imagination depends on its independence from actuality. The products of the image-making power must express freedom from the limits of the condition of the self, and, as such, they must both remain different. When images conform to the real, there is identity with the real and with the suffering experienced in that real, while "Magie" means loss of association with the real and its anguish through the freeing of the imagination from all relationship with the actuality of the event.

Magical intervention — changing the situation and not the event in order to triumph over suffering by displacing it — is continued throughout the rest of the texts of *Entre centre et absence*. The interior asset is the imagination which its proprietor projects in direct images beyond all comparisons, for comparative representations are based on points of agreement, while imaginary products have no counterpart. Release in "Une tête sort du mur" ("A Head Is Sticking Out of the Wall") comes only when he goes beyond comparisons in his desire to leave the solitude of the self; the head is rejected because it is part of outer spectacle rather than interior fancy. The head in this text is not far removed enough from reality, whereas in "Un Tout Petit Cheval" ("A Very Small Horse") the creator loses control in a moment of complete distraction and his creation, the horse, blames him for his distress: "Mais, qui est fautif en faute? Est-ce moi?" ("But, who is faulty in fault? Am I?" *PLI*, p. 19). In "Vision," he uses the value of the invention by recombining elements of the real: a man washes seventeen different arms, but he is never satisfied with any of them, so he leaves with the eighteenth arm. It is of no concern that the man and his arms are true. In fact, there is no implication that what happens is true; it is seen vividly and clearly even though the mind cannot grasp the "vision" in terms of actual existence and experience.

Other visions and projections of the imagination are found in "L'Animal mange-serrure," which, as the title indicates, treats a lock-eating animal; in "On veut voler mon nom" ("They Want to Steal My Name"), in which a mirror is used as a screen for viewing Barnabé who has three gold teeth; in "Rêve de Moore" ("Moore's Dream"), where a breast is metamorphosed into an apricot; and in "Une femme me demande conseil" ("A Woman Asks My Advice"), which is a text of pure whimsy. The past is a hindrance ("Rentrer" — "Return") to the freeing of the pure self because it reinforces identification with the fixed form of self, the center. In

"La Nature, fidèle à l'homme" ("Nature, Faithful to Man"),
Michaux criticizes the man who prefers to operate in terms of simi-
larities rather than contrasts. The attack on security through submission is accompanied by an attack on submission through regula-
tion and regularity in "Le Bourreau" ("The Executioner"). The
usual executioner does not see the act as a distinctive one because
he is accustomed to it.

Michaux's projection of the forms created by the imagination is
not limited to visual images, for it includes sound displacement and
verbal creations as well. In "Dimanche à la campagne" ("Sunday
in the Country"), words promenade as people; free use of word
play, even to the point of zaniness and incomprehensibility, annihilates all relationship with outer space because it denies definition
and identifiable content to things external. In "Quand les motocyclettes rentrent à l'horizon" ("When the Motorcycles Disappear on
the Horizon"), Michaux combines the visual and the auditory in
his praise of the rapidity of passage of the motorcycles. It is the un-
seen speed which stimulates the imagination; the event of the
motorcycles racing to the horizon remains unchanged, just as the
man who washes his arms in "Vision" remains a man; but the actual spectacle — speed in one case and proliferation of arms as non-
satisfaction in the other — is transmuted through detachment of
the self from the scene which in turn leads to control over the scene
through the liberated imagination.

The defeat of everyday suffering which characterizes existence in
outer space is similarly captured in the eight sketches which accompanied the 1936 edition of *Entre centre et absence*. These drawings
expose metamorphosis; depending on how the viewer looks at
them, they change in shape and structure, and, consequently, in
meaning. No single drawing can be readily identified, but each has
multiple identities, as the *moi* of the prose texts projects a myriad
of scenes as varying in their content as in their style. Yet what unifies the sketches is the same sensation of equilibrium which the title
and volume as a whole transmit. As neither-nor representations,
the drawings cannot be assumed to be a given rendition because of
the deliberate ambiguity imposed upon their delineation, while at
the same time there is sufficient suggestion of possible identification. For example, at first glance the frontispiece to the volume
seems to be a stylized unemotional mask with gigantic lips which
could also represent the defiant act of sticking out one's tongue. To

one side of the forehead, there is a small head which is more circular than the oval of the larger head; and this second head, devoid of mouth and nose, marked only by two blank spaces for eyes, appears detached from the first head. The separation between the two forms is slight, but still noticeable. Point of view is shifted from the larger head which occupies the center to the upper corner where the smaller head is located. Hence, the perspective alone of the drawing is between center and absence of center. Also the "eyes" are looking off the page into space, possibly into nothingness, but the viewer wonders just what these "eyes" see. The longer one studies this particular drawing, the more one's attention focuses on the smaller head and the actual center becomes a background. The smaller head may well be upside down; in fact, there do seem to be a nose and a mouth above the eyes, and the expression on the face seems to be one of wonderment. Once the smaller head becomes the center of interest, the larger head by contrast changes from the expression of defiance to one of great effort at spitting out, if not vomiting, some inner repulsive entity. As the larger head takes on more and more an attitude of expulsion, its oval shape evokes strain in its elongation; the smaller head becomes more perfect in its roundness. Indeed, the drawing becomes an expression of suffering (the elongated head in the act of discharge) which is overcome by a free-floating, imagined sphere which carries the expression of release, if not a measure of contentment. The event of suffering may remain in evidence in the sketch, but the situation is radically changed through the actual displacement of the suffering as represented by the detachment of the smaller (and more contented) head.

Similarly, a blot at the end of "Un Tout Petit Cheval" changes its stance and structure and actually takes on the shape of a horse only because it is placed at the end of a particular text. Identification based on placement is, however, crucial to the metamorphosis which occurs as the viewer examines it because the horse seems to have a life of its own, independent of its creator; the drawing becomes the projection of freedom. A scorpion at the end of "La Nature, fidèle à l'homme" continues the text beyond its printed form. In attacking security in the familiar, Michaux's sketch gives mute, but all the more dramatic, testimony to nature's infidelity to man.

The visual intensification brought about by the sketches in *Entre centre et absence* continues in *La Ralentie (Woman in Slow Motion)*. The first two paragraphs of this rather long prose text (eleven pages) originally appeared as a separate text in the 1936 edition of *Entre centre et absence*[2] and were accompanied by a sketch. The drawing can be viewed as several figures, such as an angel bird or a winged woman. In a slowed-down fashion, as the title suggests, the details are magnified so that identification with the real and the known is lost. Going beyond the normal in a tension of restraint versus freedom (definite-indefinite, center-absence), Michaux equalizes opposing forces in a visual representation of weight and aeriality, the concrete and the abstract — again, a neither-nor rendering.

The text, *La Ralentie,* expresses constraint on the one hand and exit from constraint on the other. Reviewing life in a slowed-down way brings to light the misery of experience, the anguish of daily living, and the problem of awareness of the memories which constitute the past. The female figure of the sketch in 1936 is the hope of identification with another as a means of getting out of the self; but by 1938, Marie-Lou has become Lorellou (a more sonorous name) and she is further linked to the Juana who recalls the South American experience of *Ecuador*. Nothing is gained from the review process, except perhaps confirmation of the need to be somewhere other than at center, for memories reinforce the might-have-been and augment the suffering of the present by replacing past hope with despair ("hier, croquant ma naïve espérance"—"Yesterday, crunching my naive hope," *PLI*, p. 51).

The stark realization of the horror of existence which is further intensified by memories is countered by the following section, *Animaux fantastiques (Fantastic Animals)*. The turmoil and frustration of being at center in *La Ralentie* are nullified by the calm and access to real freedom through the power of the imagination to create beyond the center in *Animaux fantastiques*. Yet fundamental to both sections is the process of intensification; but, whereas in the first case it victimizes, in the second instance it strengthens. Based on a dialectic of illness-noise and health-silence, Michaux's animals express real freedom, the ability to control anguish by projecting the fantastic: "Même les choses ne trouvent leur centre qu'en vous" ("Even things find their center only in you." *PLI*, p. 60).

The ill person in *Animaux fantastiques* is a victim who submits to others; his suffering is an intrusion which causes boredom, dissatisfaction, and uneasiness, as well as the physical discomfort caused by a disease. His impotence to assert mastery over the actual event of his suffering is reflected in the diminution of his own identity and in his lack of a personality to impose on the scene: "Impuissance, puissance des autres" ("Impotence, the power of others," *PLI,* p. 57). In this apprehensive and agitated state, noise represents intrusion from outer space; the external world preys upon the ill person and gives him no rest. But the concerns and worries which accompany illness can be countered through intensification of the frustrating intrusion of noise. Concentration on the source of dissatisfaction and discomfort magnifies them to such an extreme degree of being that anguish is transformed into a desirable situation. This magnification of noise (intrusion from outer space) so strengthens suffering that it becomes a qualitative rather than quantitative experience and moves to inner space. It becomes a possession which in turn is projected outward and nullifies the turmoil of suffering. Original order is reinstated, as the silent concentration of inner space asserts mastery over the noisy imposition of outer space.

The fantastic animals of the title are only one manifestation of the inner strength of the imagination. The ill person turns the interruptions of the external event into unreal shapes drawn from the animal world and thereby regains his health. The ensuing negation of victimization and its accompanying uproar offer a moment of serenity. At rest, calm, comfortable, motionless, and still, the convalescent counters the abnormal event of illness with the abnormal creations of inner space, the fantastic animals, and experiences freedom from subjugation. As convalescence represents the recovery of the power to control outer space, silence represents life: "Dans ce profond silence seul compatible avec son délicieux bruissement, vit la santé" ("In this profound silence alone compatible with its delicious murmuring, health exists," *PLI,* p. 63).

The power to transform the sordidness of existence in outer space is also the subject of the fourth section *L'Insoumis (The Rebel).* As the title implies, the unruly, unsubjugated personality which defies authority and rejects imposed discipline is the possessor of identification and center; yet, outer incapacity to accept jurisdiction is seen as the inner manifestation of organized resistance. By juxtaposing hell as the dreary everyday state of being a nobody with the lost paradise of splendid sleep in which being is being a someone, Michaux destroys the norms of performance in outer space. Only through the imagination can there be any successful revolt against the possible victory over the everyday stalemate of existence. The imagination overcomes defeat of confrontation with the world, for being awake is the undoing of center: "L'homme retrouve sa défaite: le quotidien" ("Man rediscovers his defeat: the everyday," *PLI,* p. 67). The inner adventure destroys the limitations of existence in the world: "Capitaine à la débâcle, il détruit les derniers échafaudagaes, il nivelle tout dans la cendre, il accomplit la ruine" ("Captain of the debacle, he destroys the last scaffoldings, he levels all into ashes, he accomplishes ruin," *PLI*, p. 67). Revolt, then, is an attitude which defeats all spatial and temporal dimensions and results in the projection of the splendor and majesty of inner terrain.

Projection of the imagination as a revolt against the everyday is found in *Je vous écris d'un pays lointain (I Am Writing to You from a Faraway Land)*. The verb, *écrire (to write),* closes distance between the inner space of the imagination *(pays lointain)* and the real, as it actualizes inner desires and changes the form of outer space. The *je* of the title is the feminine writer of the twelve observations which compose the text. She is the imagination as author-creator who jots down her impressions of inner terrain. The *vous* is first the textual recipient of the written communication, the reader within the fiction of the text, as well as the actual reader of the text. Hence, Michaux annihilates all distance between creator and creation, author and reader, as he moves to a predominant *nous (we)* form at the end which not only draws the actual reader into identification with the in-text reader, but also involves the reader with the problem which concludes the text: "Quand allons-nous nous voir enfin?" ("When are we finally going to see one another?" *PLI,* p.80). And, indeed, this question sums up Michaux's artistic exploration throughout *Lointain intérieur* and provides the springboard for his subsequent imaginary travels in *Ailleurs (Elsewhere).*

While Michaux is concerned with giving concrete form to the imagination, he is more interested in reversing the pattern of existence through the continual projection of the imagination. When will the imagination and its proprietor see (know) each other? When will the reader and the poet-creator meet? The act of writing represents one way of seeing inner desires actualized. The things noted in this faraway land are in themselves insignificant and meaningless; their presence in writing is testimony tó their existence, not to their definition in outer space terms. The sea cannot advance because of the sea which limits it, clouds cannot be caught, mountains are obstacles to walking, and shivers are not educated to respond in given situations. None of these observations is so fantastic as to be incredible, for Michaux remains in contact with existing phenomena. The very form adopted for the presentation of the text, a travelogue — a series of short letters which one might write to a foreign pen-pal — is orthodox, even ordinary. There is no question as to the authenticity, historicity, or validity of the writer's observations. The writer is casual in her description of things, yet selective as though she is trying to convince the reader that a visit to her land would be of interest: "Vous n'imaginez pas tout ce qu'il y a dans le ciel, il faut l'avoir vu pour le croire" ("You can't imagine all there is in the sky, it must be seen to be believed," *PLI*, p. 79). By the end of *Je vous écris d'un pays lointain*, the faraway seems near indeed.

As if to demonstrate the closing of distance through the act of writing, the section of thirteen *Poèmes* which concludes *Lointain intérieur* reemphasizes the use of the imagination for the realization of inner desires, and the poem itself, as a generic form, emerges as the point of conjunction between center and absence: the poem becomes the expression of Eureka, triumph at the discovery of the pure self through the imagination.

The publishing history of these thirteen poems gives insight into Michaux's practice of emergence-resurgence. Four were originally included in *Entre centre et absence*[3]; in *L'Espace du dedans*, five of the 1938 and 1963 *Lointain intérieur* poems are listed as *Plume* texts and four as *Entre centre et absence* poems, while only three appear as belonging to *Lointain intérieur*, and, of those three, two were originally in the 1936 edition of *Entre centre et absence*. Hence, Plume, Michaux's first sustained fictitious character, is part of the "faraway inside," and the use of the poem as opposed to narrative prose emerges as the transitional form from volume to volume and ultimately provides unity among all of Michaux's texts. The poems are concise outward projections of the power of the imagination to overcome the world, and, through poems, Michaux epitomizes the discoveries of his inner explorations.

In "Repos dans le malheur" ("Rest in Misfortune"), Michaux

finds misfortune necessary for action. It is not absurd and it does
not represent submission, for the process of inversion, which is a
preferred Michaux operation, makes *malheur* a confirmation of
existence. Misfortune is one possession which leads to an appreci-
ation of moments of calm and non-motion. The repose of the title
has meaning only because it stands for a moment during which opposition is abandoned; rest is recognition of the positiveness of being free, and freedom cannot be known without the experience of
non-freedom. The possessive *mon* which appears throughout the
text ("mon grand laboureur . . . ma vraie mère . . ." — "my great
ploughman . . . my true mother . . .," *PLI*, p. 83) affirms misfortune as an asset for the stimulation of the imagination. In a similar
vein, "Mon Sang" ("My Blood") confirms the individuality and
particularity of one's inner resources.

Just as "Repos dans le malheur" and "Mon Sang" confirm life
and activity, so does "Sur le chemin de la Mort" ("On the Road to
Death"), in which the mother is transformed into a beautiful young
girl at the moment of the cessation of life. Death is seen as a stop-
ping place on the natural road of activity; while it may not be com-
prehended, it is neither feared nor resented. Death is the impenetra-
ble Opaque, a nothingness, which is distinguished from life only by
the inner circulation of forces which generate awareness of one's
vulnerability to attack in outer space. As the mother's tears are
turned into a gracious smile, which verges on the impishness of the
very young, she is freed from the anguish of the defeat of the everyday. In the following text, "Paix égale" ("Even Peace"), Michaux
continues this theme, except that here life is viewed as a flower
which opens up only to be beaten by the elements; the bloom must
close its corollas of anguish ("FERMEZ vos corolles d'angoisse!"
PLI, p. 87) in order to protect itself.

Withdrawal into the self as the only terrain on which the self is
the self is reflected in "Pensées" ("Thoughts") and "Vieillesse"
("Old Age"). "Pensées" are the fragments which confirm the multiplicity of existence and affirm outer space. Thoughts are gener-
ated by awareness of the world at large in contrast to thinking (*penser*) which Michaux equates with *vivre*, to live as inner motion be-
low the surface. "Vieillesse" continues the attack on mental confrontation with outer space, for all efforts at being engaged in the
world lead to plurality, contradiction, and disillusionment
("Vieillesse, veilleuse, souvenirs: arènes de la mélancolie! Inutiles

agrès, lent déséchafaudage!'' — ''Old age, sentry, memories: arenas of melancholy! Useless fittings, slow dismantling of the scaffolding!'' *PLI*, p. 89).

Frustration at being unable to unite inner and outer space is captured by ''Le Grand Violon'' (''The Great Violin''): ''Mon violon est un grand violon-girafe'' (''My violin is a great giraffe-violin,'' *PLI*, p. 70). The use of a musical metaphor as an organizing image and its extension into the animal world generates a gamut of emotions; sounds run up and down the long neck, entering the body just as vibrations enter the player's body. Yet, the great violin literally unites the physical body of the musician with the wood which composes it and at the same time defies true fusion, for the player remains separated from his instrument: ''. . . je me retourne sur lui, inquiet, pris de remords, de désespoir, / et de je ne sais quoi, qui nous unit, tragique, et nous sépare'' (''. . . I turn back to it, worried, seized with remorse, with despair, / and with I don't know what, which unites us, tragic, and separates us,'' *PLI*, p. 91). In the same way, the poet is tied to, yet apart from, the outward projection into concrete form of his inner desires, as in the two following texts, ''Dans la Nuit'' (''In the Night'') and ''Télégramme de Dakar'' (''Telegram from Dakar''). In both poems, one word takes over through repetition and becomes the autonomous vibration of meaning without any reference to external or internal association. In ''Dans la Nuit,'' there is syntactical movement from the preposition of physical location, *dans (in)*, to a preposition of possessiveness, *à,* to an independent existence marked by the omission of the definite article *la*, to an all-inclusive and encompassing nature, indicated by the preposition *sous,* and finally to an absolutized form of the formless Night, ''La Nuit.'' Similarly, the word which eventually takes over in ''Télégramme de Dakar'' is ''baobabs,'' which visually dominates the African landscape to the point that these trees become the communication (telegram) which evokes all of Dakar.

Just as baobab emerges as the sensation rather than the idea which dominates ''Télégramme de Dakar,'' so in ''Mais Toi, quand viendras-tu?'' (''But When Will You Come?'') the quality of the emotion takes precedence over the idea through Michaux's attention to adjectives rather than to nouns. The last line of this text, ''Dis, Gros lot, où veux-tu donc tomber?'' (''Say, Jackpot, just where do you want to land?'' *PLI*, p. 98), questions the absolute-ness of the capitalized "Tu" and "Ta" of the first two stanzas. If the text ended after the first two stanzas, it would indeed represent a note of despair in Michaux's work: "et adieu, Michaux" (*PLI*, p. 98), but the mock humor of the last stanza presents a flippant finale to an otherwise depressing poem. In the first stanza, "Toi" appears as an absolute, and each line reinforces its sovereighty; the advent of "Toi" is unquestioned; it is only a matter of when "Toi" will come and put an end to the "ridicule univers" inhabited by the poet. The poet even admits his defeat ("Je désespère vraiment" — "I truly despair," *PLI*, p. 97) and seeks the dissolution of his identity and odious existence: "me projetant non comme homme / mais comme obus dans la voie verticale / TU VIENDRAS" ("Hurling myself not as a man / but as a shell into the vertical path / YOU WILL COME," *PLI*, p. 97).

Apprehension of the inevitable end in stanza one, however, is not so forcefully maintained in stanza two: "Tu viendras, si tu existes" ("You will come, if you exist," *PLI*, p. 97). Perhaps, indeed, "Toi" is not death, for the adjective *appâté (lured)* in the second line appears in the masculine form; as a qualifier for "tu," "tu" cannot be death which is feminine in French ("la mort"). The reader's search for a textual masculine reference — and *appâté* is the only adjective in the entire text which describes "tu" (all others are used in the feminine form as attributes of a feminine quality which evokes "tu" as in *présence, cathédrale, démesure*) — leads only to "Gros lot" at the end. Doubt about "Tu's" advent in the second stanza is further reinforced by the artistic power play which asserts the poet's ability to initiate order and end fragmentation: "Jetant mon allumette dans Ta démesure" ("Throwing my match into Your excess," *PLI*, p. 98). The match has the potential to start fire; it is not passive, but represents the active election of poetic consummation: "et adieu, Michaux." In the second stanza, the autobiographical reference negates the despair of the preceding lines. Death ends life; it does not end identity. The snuffing out of Michaux is not the snuffing out of existence, but the ending of the "pensées-images" ("thought-images") which have prevented him from becoming free to discover and express the pure self.

The last stanza confirms the fact that the text is neither a metaphysical statement nor a desire for ending a life of deception. If anything, it elects deception as caprice in its questioning of absolutes beyond the self: "Ou bien, quoi? / Jamais? Non? / Dis, Gros lot, où veux-tu donc tomber?" ("Or else, what? / Never? No? / Say, Jackpot, just where do you want to land?" *PLI*, p. 98). The conversational tone of this final stanza refutes the serious musings of the first and second stanzas. Secondly, every line ends with a question which repudiates the declarative tone of the first two stanzas. Thirdly, the acceptance of playing, literally rolling the dice, is assertive of the self: the poet is willing to toss his match or spark of creative energy and see what happens. *Tomber (to land)* here belongs, of course, to the vocabulary of gambling. The "Gros lot" ("Jackpot") then refers not only to the "Tu" of the title, but also to Michaux himself; if the "tu" can be separated from Michaux, it can be said to represent his source of inspiration, but no more: "sortant de l'ether, de n'importe où, de dessous mon moi bouleversé, peut-être" ("coming out of the Ether, from anywhere, from under my upset self, perhaps," *PLI*, p. 98). Hence, "Mais Toi, quand viendras-tu?" must be seen as a text on art, which presents Michaux as the poet who, in his adventure to a non-personal world where there is no pain and despair, is willing to take a chance on the possible loss of self. Overcoming despair in order to liberate the pure self is a victory, as Michaux challenges established order.

Defiance is also the main theme of "Comme pierre dans le puits" ("Like a Stone in the Well"). As a stone disturbs the calm stagnant water in the well, Michaux affirms his own independence and criticizes those who philosophically (and thereby abstractly) think they are in revolt but are not: "Camarades . . . mais il n'y a pas de camarades du 'Non,' / Comme pierre dans le puits mon salut à vous! Et d'ailleurs, Zut!" ("Comrades . . . but there are no comrades of 'No,' / Like a stone in the well my greeting to you! And moreover, Heck!" *PLI*, p. 100). Refusal to go along with his philosophical time[4] which justifies certain acts because they may contribute to a better future, is continued in the long free verse text "Avenir" ("Future"). It does not matter what knowledge may be available in the future; the present is all the more oppressive because the future holds the promise of deliverance. Since the future will never understand the present agony of limitation, future men must know that they were hated in their past for not having to share the misery of knowing that oppression will end and not being part of it: "Jamais, Jamais, non JAMAIS, vous aurez beau faire, jamais ne saurez quelle misérable banlieue c'était que la Terre" ("Never, Never, not EVER, you will try in vain, Never will you know what a miserable suburb Earth was," *PLI*, p. 103). The very knowledge that present major efforts will one day be viewed as failures, if known at all, is a bitter protest against outer space confrontation.

At the end of *Lointain intérieur*, Michaux's defeat of the everyday is actualized through the dispersal of outer space and projection outward of inner space. Hence, *Lointain intérieur* precedes *Un Certain Plume* in the same volume and affirms what was only suggested in *Difficultés, Plume,* and *Le Drame des constructeurs*. It is *Lointain intérieur* which gives these works of inner explorations into the imagination a position of importance which may have otherwise escaped from view. The *Poèmes* which form the last section are dispersed between *Plume* and *Lointain intérieur* in *L'Espace du dedans* as concrete evidence of Michaux's intertextuality. The emergence of *Un Certain Plume* as part of *Lointain intérieur* testifies to Michaux's arrival at Eureka through the creative space within.

II *Elsewhere*

The years which mark the collected volume *Plume précédé de Lointain intérieur* are the same years during which Michaux composed and published his account of a real trip to Asia, *Un Barbare en Asie* (*A Barbarian in Asia,* 1933), and his imaginary voyage to Great Garabagne (*Voyage en Grande Garabagne,* 1936). These works are directly linked to the Eureka of the imagination, as are the later works, *Au pays de La Magie* (*In the Land of Magic,* 1941) and *Ici, Poddema* (*Here, Poddema,* 1946) which were grouped with *Voyage en Grande Garabagne* to form the collection *Ailleurs* (*Elsewhere,* 1948). In a new preface which he wrote for a revised edition of *Un Barbare en Asie* in 1967, the same year that *Ailleurs* was also revised and republished, Michaux rejects the voyage into the real as being unreal: "Voyage réel entre deux voyages imaginaires. Peut-être au fond de moi, les observais-je comme des voyages imaginaires qui se seraient réalisés sans moi, oeuvre d' 'autres.' Pays qu'un autre aurait inventés. J'en avais la surprise, l'émotion, l'agacement" ("Real trip between two imaginary voyages. Perhaps deep within, I saw them as imaginary trips which would have been taken without me, the work of 'others.' Countries that another would have invented. I bear the surprise, the emotion, the annoyance," *BA*, p. 14). The Asia of outer space visited between 1930 and 1931 has changed and is no longer the·real Asia. By contrast, the amusement derived from the imaginary trips to inner space remains a buffer against the real: "Mes pays imaginaires: pour moi des sortes d'Etats-tampons, afin de ne pas souffrir de la réalité" ("My imaginary countries: for me, kinds of Buffer States, in order not to suffer from reality," *P*, pp. 153–54). Hence, Michaux's voyages into the imagination are related to the refusal of external confrontation and the defeat of suffering expressed in *Lointain intérieur*, for only the imaginary trips deserve to be real.

In *Un Barbare en Asie*, Michaux recounts his trip to India, Ceylon, Malaya, China, Japan, Korea. He is a barbarian in the sense that he comes from and consequently represents a civilization which is not so ancient or perhaps so refined as the oriental. In fact, his use of the term *barbare* indicates from the outset that this travelogue is not a study[5] of Asia, its facts and conditions, but a jotting down of his observations of oriental cultural attainments and attitudes. Noting his impressions of the particularity of Asian life, Michaux makes no attempts to analyze what he sees; moreover, there is no mention of any direct influence upon him as a direct result of the experience[6]: "Ici, barbare on fut, barbare on doit rester" ("Here, a barbarian one was, a barbarian one must remain," *BA*, p. 14). Of interest only is the discovery that a different culture is, nonetheless, an ordering, no matter how different. Hence in Asia, Michaux the European is the barbarian, while in Europe an Asian may be considered one. The detached point of view which the term *barbare* further suggests is maintained from page to page, as Michaux merely writes down what he sees as he sees it.

Among the particular practices which he finds distinctive of oriental civilization are contemplative religion, non-violence, use of magic, monosyllabic chanted language, non-tragic view of death, linearity in painting rather than weight, value given to saving face, unconcern with security, emphasis on politeness and self-effacement, deemphasis on the sensual, self-discipline, respect for artisanship and the technique of artistic reproduction, love of the reasonable.[7] While no conclusions are drawn — there are, in fact, only rare comparisons between East and West — and while Michaux later expresses dissatisfaction with his observations in view of the historical and cultural changes which occurred after his visit, *Un Barbare en Asie* does establish the pattern for his accounts of imaginary trips to imaginary places: "L'histoire des peuples . . . importe peu. C'est la façon, le style et non les faits qui comptent. Un peuple . . . a en propre ses *gestes,* son *accent,* sa *physionomie* . . . ses *réflexes* qui le trahissent. Et chaque homme a la figure qui le juge" ("The history of peoples . . . matters little. It is the manner, the style and not the facts that count: A people . . . possesses its own *gestures,* its *accent,* its *appearance* . . . its *reflexes* which give it away. And each man has his face which judges him," *BA*, p. 214).

While the voyage into the real is in retrospect an illusion ("il manque beaucoup à ce voyage pour être réel" — "this trip lacks a lot to be real," *BA*, p. 14), the 1933 postface on Bouddha contains an exhortation to inner space which becomes the structural pattern in the three works of *Ailleurs:* "Ne vous occupez pas des façons de penser des autres. / Tenez-vous bien dans votre île à vous" ("Do not concern yourself with how others think. / Hold to your own island," *BA*, p. 233). The return from a voyage into the real initiates the return to the inner terrain of *Mes Propriétés*, its first outward projection in the form of a sustained character in *Un Certain Plume,* its continued adventure beyond the self in *Lointain intérieur,* and its final infrastructures in *Voyage en Grande Garabagne, Au pays de La Magie,* and *Ici, Poddema*: The Eureka of Elsewhere.

In the preface to the revised edition of *Ailleurs* (1967), Michaux affirms liberation of the imagination:

Ces pays, on le constatera, sont en somme parfaitement naturels. On les retrouvera partout bientôt . . . Naturels comme les plantes, les insectes, naturels comme la faim, l'habitude, l'âge, l'usage, les usages, la présence de l'inconnu tout près du connu. Derrière ce qui est, ce qui a failli être, ce qui tendait à être, menaçait d'être, et qui entre des millions de "possible" commençait à être, mais n'a pu parfaire son installation (These countries, it will be noted, are in fact perfectly natural. They will soon be found everywhere . . . Natural as plants, insects, natural as hunger, habit, age, usage, usages, the presence of the unknown right near the known. Beneath what is, what almost was, what tended to be, threatened to be, and which among millions of "possibles" was beginning to be, but was unable to complete its establishment, *A,* pp. 7-8).

Michaux's repeated use of the qualifier *naturel* deserves attention, for it seems to exclude the notion of the imagination as the power to create what has never been seen and, consequently, as the means to change life and transform the world. On the other hand, *naturel* for Michaux cannot be separated from the power of the imagination to relieve the tedium of the real, for the imagination gives form to what coincides with the essence (inner terrain) of its proprietor. Hence, the imagination and the forms it takes are natural, normal in that they do not deviate from what is in agreement with one's inner space. The three countries evoked in *Ailleurs* are natural because they are familiar to the one who has traveled to them, and they remain natural years later (as opposed to the later unnaturalness of the trip to Asia) because their point of origin is inward, while their outward form is that of a translation of natural appetites, instincts, and desires — natural because they belong to inner space: "Il [l'auteur] s'y est trouvé plus à l'aise qu'en Europe. C'est déjà quelque chose" ("The author found himself more at ease there than in Europe. That is already something").[8]

In *Voyage en Grande Garabagne,* Michaux's prose reflects the same detached attitude of observation and the noting of cultural practices and attainments as in *Un Barbare en Asie.* In fact, the customs of the particular civilization of Garabagne are no more alien to a European than those of Asia. No fewer than thirty-seven tribes are visited (Hacs, Emanglons, Omobuls, Orbus, Ecoravettes, Ossopets, Mastadars, Nans, Halalas, Hivinizikis, etc.), while several distinct geographical places (cities, provinces) are described: Orpdorp, Kivni, Nadnir, Ormz, Hebbore. Great Garabagne is a full civilization with its own geography, ethnic groups, government, mores, social classes, beliefs, traditions, literature, music, amusements, architecture, animals, religion, and temperament. In short, Great Garabagne is a nation in anthropological and ethnological terms, but its creation is not a formulation of an ideal country; rather, Great Garabagne is conjured up as a counterbalance to the real. In Great Garabagne, there are oppressions, injustices, and inanities, which are, if anything, even more absurd than the habits and customs practiced in the real world: "En voyage, où presque tout me heurte, ce sont eux (Etats-tampons) qui prennent les heurts, dont j'arrive alors, moi, à voir le comique, à m'amuser. Mes 'Emanglons,' 'Mages,' 'Hivinizikis' furent tous des personnages-tampons suscités par le voyage" ("On a trip, where nearly everything jostles me, the Buffer States are the ones who take the bumps, which I end up seeing as funny and laughing at. My 'Emanglons,' 'Magis,' 'Hivinizikis' were all buffer-characters created by travel," *P,* p. 154). In order to cope with the suffering of existence in outer space which is intensified by travel, Michaux turns to inner space (Great Garabagne) and negates actual suffering in freeing the pure self through the imagination. He does not change, alter, or transform outer space, but he does make it liveable by venting his desires, appetites, feelings, instincts through art.

While *Voyage en Grande Garabagne* relates to Michaux's Asian trip (as earlier *Plume* was tied to his trip to Turkey), *Au pays de La Magie* represents his reaction to a visit to Brazil: "Ainsi les mages (*du Pays de la Magie*) furent commencés le lendemain de mon arrivée à Rio de Janeiro, me séparant si bien de ces Brésiliens, avec qui je ne trouvais pas le contact" ("Thus the Magi [of the *Land of Magic*] were begun the day after my arrival in Rio de Janeiro, cutting me off so well from those Brazilians, with whom I couldn't make contact," *P,* pp. 154-55). In *Au pays de La Magie,* Michaux indulges his imagination by appealing to the reader's inner space. Destruction of logical, rational norms through a rational demonstration of the fantastic closes the distance between the real and the imagined, the reader and the text. For example, Michaux evokes walking simultaneously on both banks of the same river, water which does not flow, fires that are neither hot nor burning, water shepherds, a wound in a wall, peace among the animals. Such fantastic distortions shock the reader into reacting without reflection and provoke the reader into an unwilled response (impulse, appetite) to the text. Once the reader accepts the overthrow of the familiar order of logic, the events become understandable: near its source, it is possible to walk on two banks of a river at the same time; stagnant water does not flow; fireflies are neither hot nor burning; fishermen are water shepherds. The essential point, however, does not reside in the possibility of explanations, but in Michaux's ability to shock the reader out of imposed ways of thinking and to compel him to experience the elsewhere: "Mais il s'agissait toujours de l'impossible, de rendre le lieu sans lieu, la matière sans matérialité, l'espace sans limitation" ("But it was always a question of the impossible, of making the place placeless, matter immaterial, space limitless," *E-R,* p. 95).

Similarly in *Ici, Poddema*, Michaux journeys into the

imagination in order to free the self from an external situation. The disordered culture depicted in Poddema-Ama and Poddema-Nara is summed up at the end of the work as metamorphosis: "Vous avez vu Poddema sous un signe. Elle a vécu sous d'autres. Elle vivra sous d'autres encore. Métamorphose! Métamorphose, qui engloutit et refait des métamorphoses. Chez nous, un moment ouvre un océan de siècles" ("You have seen Poddema under one sign. It has lived under others. It will live under still others. Metamorphosis! Metamorphosis, which engulfs metamorphosis and creates new ones. With me, one moment opens an ocean of centuries," *A*, p. 240). Poddema's civilization is no stranger than the anthropological organizations described in *Ecuador, Un Barbare en Asie,* and *Voyage en Grande Garabagne.* By unstructuring accepted form, Michaux negates outer space and forces the reader to accept instinctively and instantaneously the projection of inner space, which is Poddema. Metamorphosis, then, is not the change and mutation of an external form presented to view; rather, in Michaux's world, metamorphosis occurs inwardly, and, in *Ici, Poddema,* as well as in all of *Ailleurs,* the destruction of reader norms projects the reader not outward, but inward. *Ailleurs* does not open up the world in a new form; it closes out the world. The world is not transformed; it ceases to exist, to intrude, to constrain. The Elsewhere of the reader's inner terrain emerges naturally, and with value, because it is his real world, the one in which his desires are in accord with their expression and release: Eureka!

CHAPTER 5

To Paint a Poem

J'ÉCRIS pour me parcourir. Peindre, composer, écrire: me parcourir. Là est l'aventure d'être en vie (I write in order to get acquainted with myself. Painting, composing, writing: getting acquainted with myself. That is the adventure of being alive, *P*, p. 142).

Demonstration of the reality of man's inner terrain characterizes Michaux's work from its beginnings to the present. Every text since 1923 is in some way directed towards the liberation of the pure self and the expression of its outward projection. Consequently, all forms — verbal and visual, written and painted — abound in his work. The usage of multiple modes of expression is inherent to Michaux's view of the multiplicity of man; there is no set definition of man, just as there is no set definition of what constitutes a text. While Michaux's adoption of every form of expression may indeed give rise to his being labeled a practitioner of non-generic writing and a destroyer of form,[1] such a description tends to ignore the actual structural pattern which his non-generic technique creates. All modes, written and plastic, are not merely part and parcel of the Michaux universe; they *are* the Michaux universe, a universe which denies referentials and creates energy where there was no energy.

Energy has no form, yet it takes many forms. Energy expresses the very adventure of life because it is initial, active, and immediate. Energy is the power of self-generation of the space within. The invention of energy is what constitutes and defines art for Michaux: "Mon plaisir est de faire venir, de faire apparaître, puis faire disparaître" ("My pleasure is to bring about, to cause to appear, then to bring about disappearance," *E-R*, p. 21). His written and plastic experiments deliberately incorporate elements from known forms of expression (prose poem, verse poem, fable, story, diary, essay, aphorism, dialogue, sketch, portrait, water color, landscapes) in order to displace representative forms, to permit the birth of form, to create energy — art: "Le déplacement des activi-

76

tés créatrices est un des plus étranges voyages en soi qu'on puisse faire" ("The displacement of creative activities is one of the strangest voyages in itself that one can make," *P*, p. 83).

Bringing the life of inner space into existence destroys all obstacles of limitation in a direct transcription of the original pure self: "Un auteur n'est pas un copiste, il est celui qui avant les autres a vu, qui trouve le moyen de débloquer le coincé, de défaire la situation inacceptable . . . L'artiste est d'avenir, c'est pourquoi il entraîne" ("An author is not a copyist, he is the one who has seen before the others, who finds the way to loosen up the crunch, to undo the unacceptable situation . . . The artist is future, that is why he draws along after him," *E-R*, pp. 75-76). Michaux's invention of energy is no doubt what Rimbaud sought when he invoked the author, creator, poet figure: the self-contained work of art which is initial in its stimulation of productive activity on the part of the reader-viewer. The all-inclusive work which has no reference other than its own is the Michaux text or drawing, which arises from within and activates the without. Hence, Michaux repudiates image poems ("poèmes-images") and invents action poems ("poèmes-actions"), works which give form but are not generic forms. Words and lines are not directed into patterns; rather, they generate the power to direct desires and bring forth inner terrain. They do not imitate outer space because they are non-reproductive: "Je ne veux non plus rien 'reproduire' de ce qui est déjà au monde" ("I also don't want to 'reproduce' anything which is already in the world," *E-R*, p. 17). Free from the external frameworks of association and definition, Michaux's written texts are actually paintings in the immediacy and totality of their transcription of inner terrain: "Pas de trajet, mille trajets . . . Dès qu'on le désire, le tableau à nouveau, entier. Dans un instant, tout est là. Tout, mais rien n'est connu encore" ("No journey, thousands of journeys . . . As soon as you want it, the painting anew, whole. In an instant, everything is there. Everything, but nothing is yet known," *P*, p. 115).

In the visual work, *Peintures (Paintings,* 1939) and its expanded edition, *Peintures et dessins (Paintings and Drawings,* 1946), as well as in the "verbal" volume, *Epreuves, exorcismes (Trials, Exorcisms,* 1945), Michaux expresses in plastic and written modes the creation of energy. In these works, in appearance so different, the poem produces a plastic vision and the plastic work generates written expression. A painting in its simplest sense is, for Michaux, a wordless phrase ("phrase sans mots"), which invents words through colors; the written text is the emerging sentence ("montée verticale") which creates visions through a hammering out of words ("martèlement des mots"). Painting and writing (*peinture* and *écriture*) are one and the same. They are means of expressing directly the energy of inner terrain where all is possible in its formless potential of activity and creation: "Ce n'est pas dans la glace qu'il faut se considérer. Hommes, regardez-vous dans le papier" ("It's not in the mirror that you must examine yourself. My fellowmen, look at yourselves in the paper," *P*, p. 89).

I *The Poet Paints*

In 1937, Michaux held his first art exhibition after only a scant dozen years of painting. The "operation" of painting (Michaux's term — instead of "technique" or "form") as a destruction of a synthetic world view and the creation of an elsewhere is not undertaken in defiance of language and literature. On the contrary, its attraction lies in its being between center and absence: a dispersed concentration which acts on inner space in its original instinctive, pre-imagined personality:

> La peinture est une base où on peut commencer à zéro (Painting is a base where one can begin at zero, *E-R*, p. 70).

> Dans la peinture, le primitif, le primordial mieux se retrouve (In painting, the primitive, the primordial is best rediscovered, *E-R*, p. 18).

These and other statements do not deny the success of the discoveries through the operation of writing. Rather, Michaux finds painting less restrictive than writing because his formation is verbal. Plastic art is the operation of displacing his own energy in one general mode of expression (the written) by another (the visual). His writing prior to his first attempts to paint has a highly visual quality: the very plasticity of Plume, for example, suggests the work of a painter; the use of drawings in *Entre centre et absence* as complements to the written text indicates the inseparability of plastic art and written work. Selection of form for expression is never more than a minor concern in Michaux's universe; on the contrary, form and expression, or experience and its communication, are so interdependent and so reciprocal that all distinction between painting and writing ceases to exist. The Michaux artistic adventure is the creation of a poetry of inner life which is all-inclusive, self-sufficient, and totally free. It is emergence and resurgence beyond the self:

> Art qui n'a pas à appréhender les contradictions du dehors . . . Art des désirs, non des réalisations. Art des générosités, non des engagements. Art des horizons et de l'expansion, non des enclos. Art dont le message partout ailleurs serait utopie. *Art de l'élan* . . . L'élan est primordial, qui est à la fois appétit, lutte, désir (Art which does not have to worry about contradictions from without . . . Art of desires, not of realizations. Art of generosities, not of commitments. Art of horizons and of expansion, not of enclosures. Art whose message everywhere else would be utopian. *Art of élan* . . . Elan is primordial, which is simultaneously appetite, struggle, desire, *P,* p. 185).

Peintures (1939) is Michaux's first published edition of his own art work. Consisting of seven poems, sixteen drawings, and introductions by Louis Cheronnet and Michaux, this volume was expanded to include forty-three drawings in the 1946 edition, *Peintures et dessins.* However, there are two major differences between these two volumes. First, the seven texts of *Peintures* are original to that work and there are no original poems in the expanded volume, which also omits one poem ("Paysages"—"Landscapes") and abridges three others. Hence, the 1946 edition contains only three complete poems ("Combats," "Couché"—"Lying Down," and "Prince de la nuit"—"Prince of Night") from the original work. Second, the 1939 work includes at the end eight black and white drawings on the righthand pages, while the left-hand pages are left empty; no printed word accompanies these drawings. In the 1946 edition, all forty-three drawings are accompanied by at least part of a written text. Regardless of these differences, however, both works demonstrate graphically the interrelationship of the poem and the painting in their revelation of the power of the inner terrain to generate an elsewhere beyond the confines of the self. Both volumes testify to the immediate experience of the imagination: "Il [Michaux] est et se voudrait ailleurs, essentiellement ailleurs, autre.

Il l'imagine. Il faut bien qu'il l'imagine" ("Michaux is and would
like to be elsewhere, essentially elsewhere, another. He imagines it.
He has to imagine it").[2]

Michaux describes *Peintures* as another window ("fenêtre") to
the inner journey, but this particular window brings into focus, as
no previous work, the actual invention of the elsewhere: "Michaux
peint curieusement sur des fonds noirs, hermétiquement noirs. Le
noir est sa boule de cristal. Du noir seul il voit la vie sortir. Une vie
toute inventée" ("Michaux paints curiously on black backgrounds,
hermetically black ones. Black is his crystal ball. From black alone
does he see life emerging. A completely invented life").[3] The relationship of Michaux's inventions in *Peintures* to the nightmare of
the approach of World War II in Europe cannot be ignored. The
intolerable world of confrontation is opposed throughout the
poems and paintings, which are, in fact, effective interventions that
neutralize the outer space situation: "En attendant, viennent
quelques personnages et des têtes irrégulières, inachevées surtout"
("In the meantime, a few characters and some irregular heads, especially unfinished ones, appear," *E-R*, p. 22).

Heads are, indeed, the unifying factor throughout *Peintures,*
even in the text "Paysages." But these Michaux heads are not portraits, for portraits conform to and describe the external situation.[4]
Rather, Michaux evokes inner space: "Je voulais dessiner la conscience d'exister et l'écoulement du temps" ("I wanted to draw the
awareness of existing and the flow of time," *P*, p. 197). Hence,
Michaux renders what he terms the portrait of temperament ("le
portrait du tempérament"), a writing which remains in motion as it
surges forth from the original terrain of life, "L'espace du
dedans": "Dans tous les inachèvements, je trouve des têtes...,
rendez-vous des moments, des recherches, des inquiétudes, des
désirs, de ce qui fait tout avancer . . . Tout ce qui est fluide une fois
arrêté devient tête. Comme têtes je reconnais toutes les formes im-
précises" ("In all incompletions, I find heads . . . , *rendezvous of
moments,* of investigations, of concerns, of desires, of what makes
everything go . . . Everything that is fluid, when it no longer
moves, becomes a head. As heads I recognize all imprecise forms,"
E-R, p. 22).

Fluidity and imprecision of detail mark both *Peintures* and
Peintures et dessins. In fact, the actual arrangement of *Peintures et
dessins* shows Michaux's work moving from the first pastel of a

fish ("La Paresse"—"Laziness"), which is imitative and reproductive of the real world, to greater and greater abstraction, obscurity, and incompleteness in his drawings. Gouaches are replaced by drawings, as the figures lose weight and become more fluid.

In this perspective, the Michaux use of the term *peinture* takes on specific definition; it refers to a completed work in which there is definite ordering and a rather all-inclusive disposition of the details; painting includes pastels, water colors, gouaches. In contrast, *dessin* means drawing in its literal sense: an outline, which gives only the main contours of a figure or object. The "paintings" in *Peintures et dessins* are placed at the beginning of the work, numbers one to twenty-nine, while the remaining fourteen (numbers thirty to forty-three) are "drawings." Hence the title of the volume distinguishes the two modes of plastic expression. On the other hand, the 1939 *Peintures* are paintings, characterized by their weight, enumeration of details, exactitude in the execution of their fullness. While incompletion and fluidity are present in *Peintures,* this work is only the beginning of this evolution in Michaux's work, and the 1946 volume marks the adoption of fluidity in its effacement of details. A *peinture* has a closed quality, for the details remain somewhat indicative of outer space, while a *dessin* is open in its invitation to follow where one may. Despite overt relationships with the external world of event, situation, and confrontation, *Peintures* is Michaux's first consistent work which generates its own creative energy from within, as well as his first work in which graphic expression dominates the written mode.

While the seven texts in the 1939 volume *Peintures* are commentaries on a specific moment, the advent of World War II,[5] they represent, nonetheless, a transcription of the turmoil of the inner state when its autonomy is threatened by external circumstances. In "Têtes" ("Heads"), the sense of foreboding of these "sorties de l'obsession" ("flights from obsession") signals an SOS: the impending loss of freedom because of an outer necessity is eerily captured by a large dark head which, "morne et gelée, considère le destin" ('dismal and frozen, considers destiny," *EED*, p. 247).[6] The whole problem of man's future is further evoked in "Clown," in which Michaux paints the clown as a large oval head, with its mouth wide open in an expression of horror; in the forehead, there is the impression of a death's head. This grotesque "portrait" of man's futile efforts to mask his inner desires of wanting the elsewhere is reinforced textually by key terms whose very sound (the initial *r*) indicates irregular movement: *risée (laughing-stock), rosée (dew), ras (flat), risible (laughable)*. Hence, the paradoxical nature of the clown is to cause amusement through his outer gestures and appearance, while his inner terrain struggles to throw off the mask. In a curious mixture of satire and buffoonery, Michaux attacks form: "Par une totale dissipation-dérision-purgation, j'expulserai de moi la forme" ("Through a complete dissipation-derision-purgation, I shall expel form from myself," *EDD*, p. 249). Terms of energy are invoked in order to render a purgation from the unformed within to the formed without (mask), as the clown's open mouth releases his aspiration to gain a nourishing space ("l'espace nourricier"), where he can begin again ("à nouveau") in a state of nothingness: "ouvert moi-même à une nouvelle et incroyable rosée / à force d'être nul" ("I too open to a new and unbelieveable dew / through being a non-entity," *EDD*, p. 250). However, in a painfully pessimistic conclusion which is further strengthened by the grotesque head in the drawing, the clown will remain laughable: "et ras . . . / et risible. . ." ("both flat . . . / and laughable. . . ,"*EDD*, p. 250). The final ellipsis reinforces the circular impasse which man's exaggerated sense of identity and role-playing have created. "Clown" is one more head which threatens a stoppage of fluid formation.

Threats of halting the energy necessary for gaining the elsewhere are also found in "Paysages" ("Landscapes"), which depict the various scars that lacerate and yet delineate the formed being. Death, the only release from these roads of a life of confrontation in outer space, is the "Prince de la Nuit" ("Prince of Night") whose immobility on a brown throne against a black background dappled with blue, green, and red stars intensifies the ridiculousness of life. The rigidity of the prince who resembles a legendary Aztec god satirizes the sterility of Europe in 1938. In "Dragon," another mythological creature recalls the need for aggressiveness: "Ainsi donc je livrai bataille pour moi seul, quand l'Europe hésitait encore, et partis comme dragon, contre les forces mauvaises, contre les paralysies" ("Hence I waged battle for myself alone, while Europe still hesitated, and set out like a dragon against evil forces, against paralyses," *EDD*, p. 252). The splashing of the water by the dragon's immense and lethal tail reflects the release of energy. The power to create is graphically rendered by the vari-colored protoplasmic shapes which illustrate "Combats"; as they move irregularly across a black background, these elastic shapes — the seeds of the future through counteraction (combat) — contrast with the fixity of the painting of the "Prince de la Nuit." The dark void in "Combats" is the fluid formlessness from which all things are invented: the black crystal ball. As a creative power surges from the black of non-form, man's elsewhere surges from his inner space. In "Couché," the prone human figure raises his head and conjures up other figures around him; the interior gesture undoes the clownish, grotesque real: "Couché / . . . pour connaître / . . . / pour défaire, pour demain / . . . couché-Pharaon" ("In bed / . . . in order to know / . . . / in order to destroy, for tomorrow / . . . a recumbent Pharaoh").

Michaux's transcription of the limitlessness of energy in *Peintures* is reinforced by his use of man's own inventive images from his past (clown, Aztec god, dragon). Whenever faced with an outer threat to his existence, man conjures up a countering energetic force from within: his imagination — not his reason — makes the situation "reasonable." Hence, however ridiculous ("risible") he may be and however inane his means of traveling the landscapes of life may be, in bed, at night, he is free to combat the day by imagining that he is regal, the king of his own inner terrain. Displacement of the real through intervention — painting — negates the outer fixity of set definitions: "mots-pensées, mots-images, mots-émotions, mots-motricité" ("word-thoughts, word-images, word-emotions, word-motivity,"[7] *P*, p. 83). The diminution of verbal primacy in *Peintures* results in the direct reader-viewer experience of the poem-action (*poème-action*). Because description is replaced by the transcription of the inner flow of energy, the within is not only exteriorized, but also concretized.

The expulsion of form through the dissipation-derision-purgation gesture in "Clown" becomes the Michaux visual journey, if not his actual operation, throughout *Peintures et dessins*. The curious arrangement of the drawings with their accompanying legends denies engagement of the reader in the written word by demanding disengagement from outer space: "Le meilleur de lui [l'homme] qui est hors de lui, pourquoi ne serait-il pas picturalement communicable? Dans la joie, l'enthousiasme, l'amour, l'élan combatif, l'exaltation de groupe, il est hors de lui. C'est là qu'il faudrait le peindre. Même sa méfiance est autour de lui"

("The best of man which is outside of him, why couldn't it be pic-
torially communicable? In joy, enthusiasm, love, combative impe-
tus, community excitement, he is frantic. That's how he should be
painted. Even his mistrust is around him," *P*, p. 100). To paint
man's space, Michaux has the legend, which in all but three cases
consists of only a few lines from one of his texts, printed on tissue
paper in red ink — red because it evokes the color of blood, life,
which screams to be released: "Les rouges surtout, pour crier, crier
malheur, crier détresse, crier délire, crier tout ce qui crie à ce moment et veut se jeter au-dehors . . . cela vient en criant, voilà ce qui
m'importe" ("Reds especially for shouting, shouting misfortune,
yelling distress, yelling delirium, screaming everything that is now
screaming outward . . . that comes from screaming, that's what is
important to me," *P*, p. 109).

Hence, while reading the legend, the painting is constantly visible
beneath the printed word. It is, in fact, impossible to read the text
without seeing the drawing, for the reading and viewing processes
are concurrent. On the other hand, it is possible to view the drawing alone by turning over the tissued words, but still the reader-
viewer can never approach the drawing without having first seen
the verbal legend. The fixity of words is literally overcome through
their placement over the plastic expression. The entity is verbal and
visual, its whole is seen in the first glance, and the interrelationship
between the two modes is based on an active exchange between writing and painting. It does not matter which mode inspired its counterpart, for, in actuality, some texts were published first and seem
to have served as the springboard for the drawings, while in other
cases the drawing may be said to have been the basis for the text.
What matters is that the colors invent words as the words create
forms. The reader-viewer is, indeed, made conscious of existence,
as Michaux generates the interior wordless phrase which presents
the without as the within: "Donner à voir la phrase intérieure, la
phrase sans mots, corde qui indéfiniment se déroule . . . ac-
compagne tout ce qui se présente du dehors comme du dedans"
("To show the inner sentence, the wordless sentence, rope which
unwinds itself indefinitely . . . accompanies everything that comes
up both without and within," *P*, p. 197). To paint a poem is to
create energy, to generate life.

II *The Painter Writes*

While it may perhaps be argued that in his equation of painting with writing in *Peintures et dessins* Michaux gives the initiative to the drawing, the fact remains that the verbal and the visual are synchronous in their expression of inner energy which refuses the hostile real. The displacement of the poet-painter's activity in his creative journey initiates a displacement of the reader-viewer's activity in confronting the page. This displacement of space between center (point of origin) and absence (no consciousness of origin) is a manifestation of the autonomy of the inner self in direct opposition to the loss of control which occurs in outer situations. The dislocation of outer space in inner energy is what Michaux terms *exorcism,* and in his *Epreuves, exorcismes (Trials, Exorcisms,* 1945) he continues to arouse man to action and deliver him from dependence on external events: "Toute situation est dépendance et centaines de dépendances . . . Une des choses à faire: l'exorcisme. L'exorcisme, réaction en force, en attaque de bélier, est le véritable poème du prisonnier" ("Every situation is dependency and hundreds of dependencies . . . One of the things to do: exorcism. Exorcism, a reaction in full force, in a battering ram attack, is the prisoner's real poem," *EE*, p. 7).

The texts in *Epreuves, exorcismes* were written during the war years (1940-1944) and represent a composite of three war volumes: *Exorcismes* (1943), *Labyrinthes* (1944), and *Le Lobe des Monstres (The Monster's Lobe,* 1944).[8] These titles express what is being released as well as the validity of the signs of deliverance. The prisoner is freed from his labyrinthine monster-making situation through a purgation which eliminates the impurities of the civilization: "Faire éclater la création. Voilà enfin une idée pour plaire à l'homme: notre réplique à la Genèse. Enfin une idée diabolique" ("Make creation explode. Finally an idea to please man: our reply to Genesis. At last a diabolic idea," *P*, p. 19). Refusal of things as they are in order to negate the despair of outer space moves the individual to ward off instability and dependency — suffering — through a rebirth of the self. The black crystal ball of *Peintures* is again at the basis of *Epreuves, exorcismes*, as Michaux goes outside (*sortir*) the real and takes the initiative in verbal signs ("épreuves") of energy which create life: exorcism.

For Michaux, the term *exorcism* participates in the lexicon of magic, but not in the usual sense of miracle-making, prophecy, or any sort of wizardry which affects human destiny. On the contrary, magic is Michaux's special term for intervention. It is simultaneously a rejection of confrontation in a situation and a positing of an offensive attitude which consciously denies actuality in its psychic release of suffering. Magic is a form of energy which purges the everyday in its refusal of the nothingness of outer space. As a counteractive measure, magic enables Michaux to attack, to become the initiator of action instead of the recipient of an act: "On peut retrouver . . . les gestes du refus et de l'attaque magique, et sinon les flammes, du moins le dur maintien de l'être momentanément galvanisé pour tenir en échec les puissances environnantes du monde hostile" ("One can regain the gestures of refusal and of the magical attack, and if not the flames, at least the hard bearing of the individual momentarily galvanized to hold in check the surrounding powers of the hostile world").[9]

While magic is strictly an inner act projected outward, humor is stimulated by an external act. Although humor may indeed generate a response from within, its base remains in the physical world. And, one of the more interesting aspects of *Epreuves, exorcismes* is the diminished, although still present and somewhat effective, role of humor as counteractive intervention. While humor may provide release, it does not affirm self-autonomy because it is a part of outer space and, as such, is dependent upon confrontation. Since humor is at times part of a situation, it is not a true expression of freedom. In contrast, magic is always a manifestation of control over the self and over the situation. It surges from the desire to intervene in the situation in order to displace it. Magic, more than humor, affirms self-independence. In "Les Craquements" ("The Cracks"), for example, Michaux finds that laughter is not enough because it is outside. His protest against stupidity, anguish, and external confusion in "L'Année maudite" ("Cursed Year"), "Lazare, tu dors?" ("Lazarus, You're Sleeping?"), and other texts are conscious assessments of the destructive character of outer space. The more man is engaged in the world and the more he tries to confront the oppressive present, the more savage he becomes and the more dehumanized the world becomes. All twenty-three sections of "La Marche dans le tunnel" ("The Walk in the Tunnel") affirm man's attempts to rationalize his confusion and distress. Meditation or reflective thought is cowardly because engagement fails to solve, much less dissolve, the harshness of the labyrinth ("Les Sphinx," "Labyrinthe," "La Lettre," "Dans la grande salle" — "In the Great Room"). Man's own weakness, his failure to assert his inner reflexes, destroys his energy ("Terrasse").

The texts which attack man's passivity and release his desires are the exorcisms, which are juxtaposed with those texts which demonstrate the possibility of activity: "Immense Voix" ("Immense Voice"), "Les Masques du vide" ("The Masks of Emptiness"), "La Paix des sabres" ("The Peace of Sabers"), "Alphabet," "Ecce Homo," and others. While the labyrinth graphically captures the fixed futility of any exit from the oppressiveness of outer space ("La prison ouvre sur une prison" — "The prison opens onto a prison," *EE*, p. 57), the only existence must be within. The series of monster poems[10] evokes growth (lobe) and activity. As the enemy (monster) grows within, it blots out the enemy without. Animation of inner creations, monsters in this case, confirms existence in "Dans la compagnie des monstres" ("In the Company of Monsters") and "La Vie double" ("The Double Life"). At the end of the volume, the limitless, undefined, formless sea ("La Mer") becomes a synonym for life. The exorcist pushes back the heavy stones which weigh man down in a tremendous exalted outburst of inner desire: "Dans le lieu même de la souffrance et de l'idée fixe, on introduit une exaltation telle, une si magnifique violence, unie au martèlement des mots, que le mal progressivement dissous est remplacé par une boule aérienne et démoniaque—état merveilleux!" ("In the very place of suffering and of the fixed idea, one introduces such an exaltation, such a magnificent violence, linked to the hammering of the words, that the progressively dissolved evil is replaced by an aerian and demoniacal ball — marvelous state!" *EE*, p. 8).

Words, then, become the exorcist's tool. As the drawings of *Peintures et dessins* surge from the black crystal ball in their creation of energy, so the writer ("Il écrit" — "He Writes") proposes a new alphabet which reduces the figure of man to his fluid essence. The two illustrations for "Alphabet" depict stick figures in a variety of positions. Arranged in the manner of an ideograph, these elongated, primitive outlines are metamorphoses of the human figure into a communications system, active in its autonomy: "Un alphabet qui eût pu servir dans l'autre monde, *dans n'importe quel monde*" ("An alphabet which could have been useful in the other world, *in any world,"* *EE*, p. 33). Michaux's ideographic alphabet brings together the written and the plastic in concrete signs which testify to the validity of magical intervention as a remedy to imperfection.

Exorcism is, of course, basically verbal in its use of oral forms to drive out evil spirits. In "Immense Voix," the first text in the volume, Michaux's use of repetition (word and sound) approaches incantation. The effect of accumulated orality is one of liberation from the actual form of the words, as the reader's consciousness takes the initiative in expelling his own breath (inner space) through the act of reading. Reading is not passive, for the word choice and arrangement do not communicate a message so much as they communicate energy, or rather, cause a release of energy. As reader-energy coincides with creator-energy, the prisoner's poem becomes the text of deliverance. Consciousness (awareness of the words as words) is metamorphosed into the conscience; self-awareness is replaced by self-assertion. The resulting peace is a stabilized neutrality, expressed in "La Paix des sabres" ("The Peace of Sabers"). Calm ("Le Calme") is born from the countering contradiction of two or more evils (sabers), just as the thread men ("Les Hommes en fil") disappear at the moment of opposition. Man's reflexes in "Voix" ("Voices") testify to the admirability of his consistent response to a history of being threatened. While his adoption of a philosophy of bondage as well as his acceptance of an era of hatred and domination are decried in "Ecce Homo," man's own history shows that he is basically unsatisfied in his role of destroyer. The problem of experience ("le vécu") and its concomitant engagement in outer space are presented in terms of chaos and confusion in "La Lettre." Thinking about disorder in "La lettre dit encore. . ." ("The Letter Goes On. . .") ultimately destroys all verbal communication ("Nous n'avons plus nos mots" — "We no longer have our words," *EE*, p. 54), as man's acts of violence become the hardened ruins of silence in "Les Sphinx."

The active immense voice of inner space can dissolve, then, outer monuments (sphinx) of passive muteness. In "Monde" ("World"), a text added to the volume in 1945, the Master of Ho offers the exit from the closed-in labyrinth of isolationism and depression: "Eloignez de moi l'homme savant . . . Le cercueil de son savoir a limité sa raison . . . Eloignez de moi celui qui s'asseoit pour penser" ("Keep the learned man away from me . . . The coffin of his knowledge has limited his reason . . . Drive away from

me the one who sits down to think," *EE*, p. 58). Thinking is passive, reflective; it is not an act: "Parlez d'abord. Parlez et vous ne
serez pas ignorant. Atteignez d'abord et vous approcherez ensuite"
("Speak first. Speak and you will not be ignorant. Get there first
and then you can draw near," *EE*, p. 58). The character, the Master
of Ho, appears in several texts: "Monde," "Le Calme," "Les
Sphinx," "Labyrinthe." *Ho* means nothing; it is literally an exclamation which expresses the release of energy from within:
"Ho!" "Hey there!" "What!" Moreover, the *o* (since the *h* is silent in French), which the pronunciation of the exclamation
forms, is graphically a mouth, the point of union between inner and
outer space. And, the sound of *o* is similar to exhalation, the release of air. The Master of Ho never hesitates to speak. In contrast,
the writer from the City of Time in "La lettre dit encore. . ." describes in capital letters the shamefulness of peace as being without
a mouth: "LA FACE A LA BOUCHE PERDUE" ("THE FACE
WITH THE LOST MOUTH"). Hence, the acceptance of form is
immobile, reflective, passive, and sterile, just as a statue's form is
static in "Annales." To refuse form is to be freed from outer control: The Master of Ho!

While the Master of Ho can easily be viewed as a comic reversal
of a Confucius philosopher figure, who, in this case, makes inane
pronouncements on conduct and attitudes — and Ho is a common
Chinese surname — it is interesting to note that Michaux never
sketches Ho. Three of the four Ho texts appear only in the 1945
edition, while the first Ho text originally served as the final text in
Labyrinthes (1944). Ho's relatively late appearance in *Epreuves,
exorcismes* must, textually, be aligned with the ordeal of exiting
from the labyrinth through exorcism. In "Labyrinthe," the theme
of no exit from the enclosure which is life ("Rien ne débouche nulle
part" — "Nothing emerges anywhere," *EE*, p. 57) is, however,
subtly moved in the 1945 edition to a position at the end of the
Exorcismes-Labyrinthes texts and just before the *Lobe des monstres* series. Placing "Labyrinthe" between the poems which indicate the way out (exorcism) and those which demonstrate what has
been purged (trials), the labyrinth itself is dissolved. The horizontal
nature of the maze is replaced by the vertical thrust ("montée verticale et explosive," *EE*, p. 8) of freedom. Ho, as a graphic and
ideographic form, becomes the visual evocation of liberation. *Ho*
also conjures up the word *haut (tall, high),* which further reinforces

the freeing of man from the flat confines of the labyrinth. In addition, as *labyrinth* suggests outer space, *ho* suggests the issue of inner space. The prisoner is indeed freed through his outburst of energy.

The reconciliation of painting and writing throughout the war years in *Peintures et dessins* and *Epreuves, exorcismes* brings about the creation of energy. As the drawings in *Peintures et dessins* become more fluid and show a deliberate effacement of detail, so the texts of *Epreuves, exorcismes* evoke an incompleteness: "Obscurité, antre d'où tout peut surgir, où il faut tout chercher" ("Obscurity, cave from which everything can come, where one has to look for everything," *E-R*, p. 28). This artistic obscurity, what Michaux terms *FANTOMISME* in his preface to *Peintures et dessins,* is plastically and verbally captured by greater and greater abstraction. The drawings in *Peintures et dessins, Exorcismes,* and *Labyrinthes* demonstrate the giving of form, rather than the reflection of form, but the imprecision of the drawings leads the viewer to complete them. In the same way, the texts of *Epreuves, exorcismes* capture the moment of freeing; they do not describe the liberation. Each reader's catharsis is an individual experience, differing in form and in expression. Energy, in terms of text and drawing, is what gives rise to form. Hence, the final text in *Epreuves, exorcismes* evokes the limitless fluctuation and movement of the sea: "Ce que je sais, ce qui est mien, c'est la mer indéfinie . . . A vingt-et-un ans . . . j'avais pensé que sur un bateau on regardait la mer. . . Tournant le dos, je partis, . . . j'avais la mer en moi" ("What I know, what is mine, is the indefinite sea. . . At twenty-one,. . . I had thought that on a boat you looked at the sea. . . Turning my back, I left . . ., I had the sea in me," *EE*, p. 108). Formless, endless, and imprecise, the sea which ends *Epreuves, exorcismes* is the black crystal ball of *Peintures et dessins.*

As shapes surge forth from Michaux's sea-crystal ball, their ambiguity effaces painting-writing distinctions. For Michaux, as for the Chinese, the same materials (pen, ink, paper) are used for painting and for writing. Similarity of medium of expression between painting and writing is further paralleled by a similarity of final effect: "Mais c'est la peinture chinoise qui entre en moi en profondeur, me convertit . . . Les lointains préférés au proche, la poésie de l'incomplétude préférée au compte rendu, à la copie" ("But it is Chinese painting which penetrates me in depth, converts me. . . Far reaches are preferred to what is near, poetry of incompleteness is preferred to the report, to the transcript," *E-R,* p. 16). The spectator verbalizes what he sees in the drawing, while the reader visualizes what he reads. Just as the drawings in *Peintures et dessins* cannot be separated from the written legends which overlay them, so the texts of *Epreuves, exorcismes* are ideographs — not only "Alphabet," but the labyrinth, the monsters, the Master of Ho, and the all-inclusive sea.

In the little known work, *Arbre des Tropiques (Tree of the Tropics,* 1942), Michaux verbally paints the character of the tropical tree. In a range of transcriptions (never descriptions of size, type, locale, color), he evokes its temperaments: blasphemer, howler, exorbitant, in a hurry. Buds, leaves, roots, branches, pistols, stamens, flowers, fruits are metamorphosed into a living presence which goes beyond its definition as tree; it is a celebration of the tree as an indicator of the elsewhere. The nineteen drawings which follow the prose text repudiate botanical description. Instead, Michaux detaches the tropical tree from the dense forest in order to let its individual gestures emerge from the page: "Il faut voir l'arbre à part, son geste. Il est tout geste" ("The tree has to be seen apart, its gesture. It is all gesture," *AT,* p. 12). As a result, each drawing shows only a part of the tree (gesture of leaves, trunk, buds), but each part suggests the whole and the spectator sees what is not physically drawn. The only drawing from this volume included in *Peintures et dessins* is typical of the sketches of the tropical tree; it is a carefully detailed pen and ink drawing of the liana which grows on the tree; the tree itself is not drawn, just the vine attached to it. Michaux actually invokes the tree by focusing on one of its parts. Throughout *Arbre des Tropiques,* the text and the drawing are inextricably interdependent. The verbal mode of the text invents the visual spectacle, just as the plastic mode of the pen and ink drawings conjures up the prose legend, and neither mode of expression is meaningful without the other.

It is significant that the final drawing in *Peintures et dessins* is one of Michaux's sketches of Plume. Here, in a black and white outline, Plume is in the shape of a large oval, which is dotted with many eyes reminiscent of the eyes of peacock feathers. The reader-spectator is brought face to face with the mirror of the artist's paper: the eyes look in turn at the reader. Originally a written form, Plume is also penned graphically. In retrospect, Plume emerges as evidence of an exorcism — projected outward, the eyes of his shapeless body act on the reader-viewer and, in so doing, the illustrated action-poem that is Plume acts and dislocates reader-viewer norms. The elsewhere is the marvelous displacement of creative activity: from the painter-poet to the page to the reader-spectator to the page. Figuratively and literally, painting and writing intervene in the real and magically exorcise the closure of the labyrinth of outer space by liberating the space within.

CHAPTER 6

The Magic of Motion

JE suis de ceux qui aiment le mouvement. . . Mouvement, comme désobéissance, comme remaniement! (I am one of those who love movement. . . Movement, as disobedience, as modification!, *E-R*, p. 65).

For Michaux, the creation of energy, its release, and the generation of motion in the space within are evidence of life itself. In his post-war works, *La Vie dans les plis (Life in Folds,* 1949), *Face aux verrous (Facing the Locks,* 1954), and *Quatre Cents Hommes en croix (Four Hundred Men on the Cross*, 1956), Michaux continues to exorcize the stagnation of outer reality with a vocabulary of change, movement, speed, circulation, power, provocation, mutation, expulsion: motion. Whereas up to the end of the war his work is dominated primarily by visual and auditory imagery, after the war his texts increase in motile images. The concentration of active words on the one hand produces texts which aggressively attack the situation of outer space in a release (exorcism) of inner dynamism. These verbal attacks are further marked by terms of negativity and dissolution, indicated by the prefixes *dé- (déplacer, défaire, désolidariser)* and *é- (éliminer, éloigner, évader)* as well as numerous negative constructions. On the other hand, the matter-of-fact tone which accompanies these combative terms gives a detached quality to Michaux's war on the paralysis of reality. His injection of invective is countered by his objective direction of rage: "Utilisation énergétique de l'ennemi de la situation irritante, du milieu hostile, du mal" ("Energetic utilization of the enemy of the irritating situation, of the hostile environment, of the problem," *P*, p. 207). The attack on the structure of the real does not create confusion. On the contrary, it eliminates disorder by uncovering the unity of inner terrain. Life is, indeed, in folds which must be straightened out (*La Vie dans les plis*), just as facing bolts and locks

to the inner domain (*Face aux verrous*) provoke the need for ways
to open them, and the revolt against the hostile situation (*Quatre
Cents Hommes en croix*) leads to the counter-anger of resistance. It
is not being which is the focal point of Michaux's work, but the
passages of being.[1]

I *Un-Structuring the Situation*

The five major sections of *La Vie dans les plis* are characterized
by passage, not by a movement from one given point to another,
but actual movement itself. The *plis* are constantly yielding to the
force of energy in an on-going disclosure of the elasticity of inner
space. Unfolding[2] the difficulties of the outer situation eliminates
the "pleats" or "wrinkles" caused by the real world and reveals in
their place the harmony of inner terrain. Michaux's very choice of
the term *plis* reflects the plasticity which he finds to be the salient
characteristic of man's essence. *Plis* does not refer to flexible objects, but, paradoxically, it is a flexible term, which can be applied
to physiological traits (wrinkles, the bend of an arm, the hollow of
a leg), to the physical condition of inanimate things (folds, marks
from a pleat), to geological features (underground undulation),
even to performance (tricks in cardgames); in addition, *plis* can be
used to indicate a protected covering or an obstacle, and it can also
be an independent object: a letter or an envelope. All these meanings can be applied to Michaux's *La Vie dans les plis,* for it is the
all-inclusiveness of the term, as its appearance in the plural further
suggests, which reveals man's ability to respond to the situation,
master it, and ultimately refuse it.

Resistance is inner revolt, indicated by the title of the first section, *Liberté d'action (Freedom of Action,* 1945). All nineteen
prose texts show an inner continuity, as the vocabulary increases in
violence from text to text in an unstructuring (*désolidariser*) of the
real. At the base of each text is recognition that there can be no
coming to terms with outer space: "Dans la vie on ne réalise jamais
ce qu'on veut" ("In life, you never accomplish what you want,"
VP, p. 12). One natural means at hand for evading the real and its
experiences of suffering is language; by giving form to inner appetites, language releases the forces beneath the folds of life and
spreads them out. The aggressiveness of the language in *Liberté
d'action* reflects what Michaux calls his "summum d'offensive," a

counter-anger ("Il faut une colère-colère" — "An anger-anger is required," *VP*, p. 35). But this rage is always directed because it is the property of its user. Man is free to act, to undo external form and its effects and assert his own essence. Consequently, the violent vocabulary is a realization of inner desires ("Les Envies satis-faites"), while the actual tone is one of calm determination.

Freedom of action necessitates first the refusal of the difficulties which abound in outer space. In the opening text, "La Séance de sac" ("The Bag Session"), Michaux recommends that all problems be placed in a paper bag and set aside; this act literally breaks up the real and liberates the imagination. Once free, there only remains the psychological adjustment to being free, which comes with practice. Michaux dedicates the remaining texts to establishing the habit of being liberated from the obstacles of the real. In a volume which reflects calculated inner continuity from text to text, Michaux deftly leads his reader from the opening hypothesis (put your problems in a bag) through an ever-increasing tempo of aggressiveness and violence in vocabulary to a final release in the last text, "Homme-Bombe" ("Man-Bomb"). This concluding text seems at first glance to turn against the reader, for Michaux announces an end to one phase of his directed efforts: "A écrire on s'expose décidément à l'excès. Un mot de plus, je culbutais dans la vérité. D'ailleurs, je ne tue plus. Tout lasse. Encore une époque de ma vie de finie. Maintenant je vais peindre" ("By writing, one definitely exposes oneself to excess. One more word and I would have tumbled into truth. Besides, I no longer kill. Everything palls. Another phase of my life finished. Now I am going to paint," *VP*, p. 46). Yet, as abrupt and perhaps as surprising as this final text to *Liberté d'action* appears, it is a manifestation of how natural is the desire to act in accord with one's own essence. Through his participation in the poet's verbal expression, the reader undergoes a psychological escape from the real and becomes in turn a bomb which can reduce the hostile real through his own creations.

While the imagery of change and dissolution which characterizes the texts of *Liberté d'action* continues throughout the next section, *Apparitions* (1946), there is a significant difference between the two. *Liberté d'action* is a verbal work which depends on the juxta-position between vocabulary and tone and on an inner arrangement which is marked by an increasing tempo. *Apparitions* begins where *Liberté d'action* ends, both in the sense of subject ("Je vais peindre''), for it is a work accompanied by drawings, and in the sense of familiarity with the freedom to act. Man is a factory (''Quelle Usine!'') for the manufacture of his own products and his own responses. While he may not be able to escape from the physical (''La Constellation des piqûres'' — ''The Constellation of Injections''), he can distort his suffering through projections of his freedom to act.

Although *Apparitions* consists of thirty-eight texts and seven drawings, it is actually constructed as a triptych: drawings, prose texts, free verse poems. The graduated continuity from text to text of *Liberté d'action* — in retrospect a reflection of the structured real which is to be unfolded — is replaced by an unstructured formal arrangement which yields to a motile unity of the visual and the verbal. The twenty-eight prose texts are topically concerned with the physical experience of pain inflicted by outer space. The vocabulary reflects actual bodily anguish and equates life with suffering. These texts emphasize the lack of peace and tranquillity, the fear of continued victimization by pain, the futility of life in the real world. The torment of such physical suffering affects even mental activities because it forces the victim to concentrate on his external personality, which is marked by pain. When man becomes conscious of his intolerable situation, he comes first to the realization that physical pain threatens the freedom to act and second to an awareness that the threat of pain and its effect of distortion are properties of the sufferer: ''J'étais dans un état surtendu, mais, sur *mon* terrain'' (''I was in an overstrained state, but, on *my* terrain,'' *P*, p. 216).

The ten free verse texts reflect a catalogue of possibilities of changing the irritating situation into a tolerable one. These texts are distinct from the prose ones, not only by form, but by the use of repetition. They are, in fact, incantations which exorcize the nightmarish suffering. Furthermore, the free verse texts in *Apparitions* are not set off by themselves as poems, which is the case in Michaux's previous works. On the contrary, the poems are placed as elements which break up the pain of the prose compositions. The first sixteen texts are in prose and strongly emphasize physical anguish and psychological frustration; the next seven are in free verse, and this grouping begins with the text, ''Apparition,'' which repeats the term *emplie (full)*. While the next twelve texts are in prose and return to the suffering expressed in the first prose group, this set reflects a diminishing effect of pain and increasing confidence *(emplie)* in the sufferer's ability to resist. Significantly, the last three texts are in free verse and capture the pushing back of anguish imposed by the real. In "Qu'il repose en révolte" ("May He Rest in Revolt"), for example, repetition of the preposition *dans*, which indicates actual physical location, affirms the victory of interior revolt, while the preposition *en*, which indicates a state or condition, appears in the title and expresses the attitude of revolt. Consequently, revolt is the psychological stance necessary to resist the real *(en)* and its realization takes place on inner terrain *(dans)*.

While the prose and free verse texts of *Apparitions* represent two different verbal panels of a triptych of *La Vie dans les plis* (the problems and their unfolding), the drawings bring the two together. The visual responses to the impositions and intrusions of the real evoke, as the volume title suggests, a distortion of the material world. Each appearance resembles a piece of ectoplasm which does not negate the existence of the physical but which, nonetheless, denies acceptance of the form of the physical. As these almost immaterial figures appear and disappear in a cinematic fade-in and fade-out manner, the spectral ensemble of the prose, free verse, and drawings moves the congested situation into a moment of repose which is possible only through inner revolt.

The ability to change the situation also serves as the underlying subject of *Portrait des Meidosems (Portrait of the Meidosems*, 1948), a work which continues to combine the visual and verbal experiences through motile imagery. While this work may seem reminiscent of *Ailleurs,* in that the Meidosems are a fictive people, *Portrait des Meidosems* is actually closer in theme and style to *Apparitions*. The twelve lithographs and sixty-nine prose sketches capture the rhythms and vibrations of energy, as the Meidosems appear, disappear, reappear, and disappear again across the page. In fact, their salient feature is the ability to fold and unfold: "Si grande que soit leur facilité à s'étendre et passer élastiquement d'une forme à une autre" ("However great their facility to stretch out and pass elastically from one form to another may be. . .," *VP*, p. 150). Always in motion, the Meidosem portrait is one of change.

Change is life, while stasis is death. The funereal atmosphere of the thirteen prose texts of *Lieux inexprimables (Inexpressible Places)* describes hell as stagnation, tillness, silence, and the lack of counterbalance. By presenting "l'enfer du séjour inchangeable" ("the hell of the unalterable stay," *VP*, p. 217), Michaux provokes the reader to posit the unexpressed: animation, sound, disruption, growth, rebellion. In the final section of *La Vie dans les plis, Vieillesse de Pollagoras (Pollagoras' Old Age)*, Pollagoras' elderly body recalls the haunted places of *Lieux inexprimables*. Old age is described as an accumulation of adversaries and a weariness of the battle to live in outer space. Worn out from the struggle to exist and from the quest for a wisdom which he never discovered, Pollagoras is now dying; his search for shelter represents his defeat by the real. As he shivers at the end of *La Vie dans les plis,* the volume comes full circle. Life is characterized by bucklings and disappointments unless freedom of action is asserted and maintained. When Michaux announces in the only text added to the collected volume in 1949, "Liberté d' action," that he will undertake no more journeys ("je ne voyage plus," *VP*, p. 23), he is proclaiming his refusal to be deceived by the real. In control of his inner terrain, he rejects the accustomed vertical position of confrontation and adopts instead the horizontal attitude of resistance. Without a directed effort to unstructure the irritating situation, life remains a series of defeats.

II   *Signs of Life*

Michaux finds that the oppressiveness of outer space lies in its structure of fixed forms, which so dictate man's acts, thoughts, and language, that they affect man's very essence. But refusal to accept the structure of the real and its inherent stasis is only the first step in opening the locks to the inner self, which consists of on-going passages of involuntary, albeit frequently conflicting, impulses, desires, and appetites. The movements within represent man's power to effect change; his multiformity and fluctuating instincts contradict the conformity of his environment. These inner gestures of the unformed (multiform) are the responses of natural energy which function in the world.

Facing the locks of form in *Face aux verrous,* Michaux turns to what he describes as "écriture directe" ("direct writing"): words themselves are locks, fixed by others in outer space for external confrontation. According to Michaux in his 1951 postface to *Mouvements,* words are fixed thoughts and reflect the architecture of the irritating situation. It is not sufficient to unstructure the situation, unless at the same time certain approaches to the situation — thoughts, words — are also eliminated. Consequently, he initiates a new language of new signs: "Non pour être complet / mais pour être fidèle à son transitoire" ("Not in order to be complete,/but in order to be faithful to its transitoriness," *M*). Signs testify to the energy of effective creation within and provoke reactions; words no longer prescribe a sign by following it, they now describe in a literal sense as "collants partenaires" ("sticking partners"): "Il faut en ce temps . . . une langue nouvelle" ("We need now . . . a new language").[3] For the generation of this new language, a thinking in signs, Michaux creates the "toile-poème" ("canvas-poem").[4]

The 1954 volume of *Face aux verrous* consists of twelve parts, most of which were published between 1949 and 1952: *Mouvements* (1950, 1951), *Poésie pour pouvoir (Poetry In Order to Be Able,* 1949), *Tranches de savoir (Slices of Knowledge,* 1950), *Le Secret de la situation politique (The Secret of the Political Situation,* 1950), *Nouvelles de l'étranger (News from Abroad,* 1952). The last, in turn, consists of seven sections which appear independently in the 1954 collected volume. Only *Fin d'un domaine (End of a Domain),* the last section, is original to *Face aux verrous.* It is significant that Michaux purposefully violates his chronology of composition and publication by placing *Mouvements* at the beginning of the work in order to emphasize thinking in signs as the way to overcome obstacles (*verrous*) to the space within. It is also important to note that the original publication of *Mouvements* marks simultaneously a decrease in Michaux's poetic productivity and an increase in his interest in painting. From 1950 to the present, Michaux has concentrated on painting and prose analyses of art, drugs, and dreams; he has published only one substantial volume of poetry, *Moments: Traversées du temps* (1973).[5]

Mouvements is, perhaps, Michaux's most inclusive work in terms of generic expression. Its composition is multiform: sixty-four pages of "taches" ("ink blots"), seven pages of a free verse poem, and a two-page postface.[6] Moreover, it has two companion pieces. The first is the 1954 essay, "Signes," in which Michaux places *Mouvements* in the perspective of his own search for a new language; the second is a work of art, *Par la voie des rythmes (Along the Path of Rhythm,* 1974), which is entirely wordless, yet not wholly a work of painting. In fact, the "toile-poème" which *Mouvements* inaugurates finds its fullest expression in *Par la voie des rythmes,* which is composed solely of the signs ("taches") which conquer the inadequacy of language.[7]

In *Mouvements,* Michaux abstracts the essence of man from his physical form: "Homme non selon la chair" ("Man not according to his flesh," *FV*, p. 10). The operation of abstraction expels the customary dimensional description of man; weight, length, geometry — in fact, all attributes of shape — are eliminated by the "taches" which are portraits of temperaments and capture the gestures of man's inner feelings: "Gestes . . . de la vie ignorée . . . de la vie impulsive . . . du défi . . . du dépassement" ("Gestures . . . of the ignored life, . . . of the impulsive life . . . of defiance . . . of going beyond," *FV*, p. 17). There is no attempt to identify the gestures; the "taches" move across the page in varying sizes and forms: "Désir qui aboie dans le noir est la forme multiforme de cet être" ("Desire which barks in the dark is the multiform form of this being," *FV*, p. 12). In his 1951 postface, Michaux admits that his purpose in *Mouvements* is to reveal man's innate energy which can change his situation. Man's inclination to change and his own changeability are found in his contradictory gestures; since man is energy — his movements — and not a fixed character of composition, he has the power to purify his own space and create his own relationships. Man's action from within, especially when it is intensified, exorcizes fear and divisiveness and releases unity.

Michaux's "toile-poème," *Par la voie des rythmes,* clearly demonstrates the efficaciousness of motion. As the viewer's eye moves from sign to sign ("taches"), he responds instinctively and involuntarily through his own feelings. The fluidity of the signs affectively brings forth pulsations and vibrations from within and evokes life itself. Rhythm, vibration, movement are indicators of motion, and motion, created by energy, is the action of living, the power of poetry. Hence, in the three texts of *Poésie pour pouvoir*, the second section of *Face aux verrous,* Michaux stresses action as the remedy to the hostile real. His rage against form takes the direction of the "poèmes-actions," exorcisms which not only expel the world of shape but which also unveil the wholeness of the self. All three poems are further characterized by repetition and the use of capital letters for key terms: "JE RAME" ("I AM ROWING," *FV*, p. 29), "EFFICACE" ("EFFICACIOUS," *FV*, p. 31), "AGIR, JE VIENS" ("TO ACT, I AM COMING," *FV*, p. 33). These three phrases, chanted throughout the texts and emphasized through the visual heightening of their topographical appearance, attack the outer situation so intensely that a single indivisible core of being is actually experienced: "Intact, comme un oeuf d'ivoire" ("Intact, like an ivory egg," *FV*, p. 35). The hard roundness of inner terrain asserts itself: "Une pensée-sentiment . . . compte vraiment et *prend un pouvoir*" ("A thought-feeling . . . truly counts and *takes on power*," *P*, p. 211). The "action de guérison" ("curing action," *P*, p. 210) opens the locks to a future of peace: *"J'ai lavé le visage de ton avenir"* (*"I have washed the face of your future,"* *FV*, p. 35). The more intense the exorcism, the stronger the experience of unity: "Ce chant te prend, / Ce chant te soulève . . . la paix rentre en toi" ("This melody picks you up, / This song stirs you up . . . peace fills you up," *FV*, p. 34).

The remaining sections of *Face aux verrous* emphasize action as the only remedy to man's situation. *Tranches de savoir (Slices of Knowledge*, 1950) is a group of 234 aphorisms which express the problem of man in the world: "Il est apparemment plus facile au tigre d'être totalement, dignement tigre, qu'il ne l'est pour l'homme, d'être homme" ("It is apparently easier for the tiger to be completely, worthily, a tiger, than it is for man to be a man," *FV*, p. 73). Man is his own worst enemy, for he is the one who fashions shapes and demands conformity to them: "Plus sur terre il y a d'hommes, plus il y a d'exaspération" ("The more men there are on earth, the more exasperation there is," *FV*, p. 81). Human security in fixed forms leads to alliances to maintain a structured outer space; men use each other in *Le Secret de la situation politique* (*The Secret of the Political Situation*, 1950), as they forge secret pacts which contribute to divide mankind.

Disagreement on adaptation to outer space and the resulting obsession to cling to given ways of thinking are the subject of all seven parts of *Nouvelles de l'étranger* (*News from Abroad*, 1952). A war is in progress in another imaginary country in *L'étranger parle* (*The Stranger Speaks)*; any passage from one part of the area to another is impossible because of the battle lines. *Quelques Jours de ma vie chez les insectes (A Few Days of My Life Among Insects)* presents another perspective of human hypocrisy and degeneracy, while *Nouvelles de l'étranger* (the subsection) evokes the vice of being so attached to the accoutrements of the outside world that permission from the State is necessary in order to die. The nine prose notations of *Personnel (Personal)* relate the unsuccessful ef-

forts to communicate the desire to leave: "Je vole après une communication qui ne peut s'établir" ("I'm after a communication
which cannot be set up," *FV*, p. 146). There is no real arrival in
travel, the cinema is limited by identification, the ringing of the
telephone is interruptive, and the situation, while changing, remains a situation. The precariousness of the real is the subject of
the prose comments of *Faits divers (News in Brief)* as well. Attempts to establish equilibrium (compass, hatchets, phials) reflect
the misfortunes of outer space confrontations. Man complicates
existence by codifying it and equating circumstances with facts. His
constant effort to adapt to his sensory impressions prevents his
imagination from establishing a genuinely definitive equilibrium:
"Comment . . . émigrer vers un réellement satisfaisant et définitif
équilibre?" ("How . . . can one emigrate toward a really satisfying
and definitive equilibrium?" *FV*, p. 159).

The three short texts of . . . *Rait*, the suffix which denotes the
conditional mood, hypothesize that the expression of disgust in
outer-space terms is a trap; only gestures, provoked by the imagination, can probably better the future. In *L'Espace aux ombres
(Space in the Shadows),* the last section of *Nouvelles de l'étranger*,
Michaux repeats the need for change in the search for center. Experiences of the past are marked by vain hopes — shadows — and
the law of domination-subordination (*FV*, p. 185), which is itself
the product of prescribed words. Michaux advocates estrangement
from this law and proposes movement to an empty space, a void,
which is free from interruptions, including the need for food, the
pursuit of pleasure, and the longing for refuge: "Savoir, autre
savoir ici, pas *Savoir* pour renseignements. *Savoir* pour devenir
musicienne de la Vérité" ("Knowledge, another knowledge here,
not *Knowledge* for information. *Knowledge* to become a musician
of Truth," *FV*, p. 189). It is knowledge of breaking free from the
ways and attitudes of the past by exorcising and releasing the inner
forces which dissolve identification with shadows and shapes: "JE
VAIS ETRE ENGLOUTIE . . ." ("I AM GOING TO BE SWAL-
LOWED UP . . .,"*FV*, p. 194). Space in the shadows is a space of
form; the void in all its intensity is the response of freedom.

Active dissolution of form and shape ends the dominion of outer
space. On the other hand, refusal to act and release inner movements ends self-reign and autonomy. In *Fin d'un domaine (End of
a Domain),* the final section of *Face aux verrous,* Michaux presents

the problem of maintaining one's freedom of motion. The first text, "Adieux d'Anhimaharua" ("Anhimaharua's Farewell"), treats the need for constant change: "J'ai marché dans la somnolence de mondes contraires . . . Deci delà mes voyages. Paix dans leurs débris" ("I have walked in the drowsiness of opposing worlds . . . From here and there in my travels. Peace in their debris," *FV*, p. 197). While intervention and the projection of the imagination into the outer situation prevents life from being too difficult to live, in "Fin d'un domaine" the proprietor runs the risk of being a slave to his possessions unless he remains free to act. Complacency, worldly involvement, and attachment to objects in "Demain n'est pas encore. . ." ("Tomorrow Is Not Yet"), "Après l'accident" ("After the Accident"), "Toujours se débattant" ("Always Struggling"), and "L'Impossible Retour" ("The Impossible Return") reinforce the role of energy in "Voilà comment elle est" ("That's How It Is") and "Dans le cercle brisant de la jeune magicienne" ("In the Disruptive Circle of the Young Magician"). The world can only be conquered through constant manifestations of energy in all its forms: rejection, reversal, filling up, clamor, rolling, liquidation.

Just as the ending of *La Vie dans les plis* returns the reader to the opening work, *Liberté d'action,* the concluding section of *Face aux verrous* impels recall of the first part, *Mouvements*. Movements are keys to the locks, which represent rigidity of form. Motion is not form, nor is it the absence of form; motion is formation, the process of creation. The magic of motion is the sign of life.

III *The Sign as Thought*

The vastness of a sign — its power to evoke and provoke motion — is dramatically captured by Michaux in a little known work, *Quatre Cents Hommes en croix (Four Hundred Men On the Cross,* 1956). This slim volume examines a traditional sign, the cross, and its contamination by the law of domination-subordination. Basically, according to Michaux, the cross is a pure sign, a simple form, but Western philosophy and conditioning demand that the cross contain the figure of a man, so that the actual sign of the cross is obscured by covering part of it with a second shape, the impure form of a crucified man. The initial purity of the cross, specifically, in this work, a Latin cross, first appears on the title page and again

on the first page, both of which are written in the shape of a cross.
Careful spacing and positioning of letters and words, as well as the
use of a wide variety of type sizes, liberate the cross form from its
stylized Christian symbolism. Once Michaux visually frees the sign,
he turns to its adapted Western form and sketches men on crosses.
The sketches, however, are by no means limited to drawings, for in
this work Michaux writes in ideograms: words are frequently so
placed on the page that their arrangement is a sketch which fuses
the verbal and the visual modes. Hence, Michaux's subtitle describes this volume as "Journal d'un dessinateur. FRAGMENTS"
("Diary of a Sketch Artist. FRAGMENTS.")[8]

While the figure four hundred is the number indicated by the
main title, the text does not treat four hundred men on crosses.
Rather, there are notations (fragments) by random numbers (#42,
#53, etc.) which represent only part of a large group of men who
have historically been crucified. In the process of looking at these
various crosses, Michaux concentrates on attitudes, positions, and
expressions and not on physical description. His examples include
the following representatives of mankind: the forgotten man, the
thief, an insect-type, a mistake, a deserter, the sufferer, the be-
trayed, the non-believer, the thinker, a quack, an angel. This mixture of the kinds of men who have been placed on the cross negates
the accepted Western notion of crucifixion as a means to salvation,
and the phrase "en croix" ("on the cross") ceases to have religious
connotations. The cross with a crucified body emerges as a repug-
nant sign, for it does not represent salvation for the one crucified or
for the onlooker ("LA MORT POUR RIEN" — "DEATH FOR
NOTHING," *QCH*, p. 12); the agony is ironic. Again, the law of
interior resistance ("LOI DES RESISTANCES INTERIEURES,"
QCH, p. 35) is expressed by Michaux in his graphic illustration of
human defilement of a pure form: "Il faudrait UN HOMME
CRISTAL" ("We need A CRYSTAL MAN," *QCH*, p. 32). The
sketches of the cross and the men on it in varying positions (to one
side, one arm hanging down) are visual exorcisms, which free the
sign from imposed images. Michaux even suggests that if seminar-
ians were made to draw crucified men instead of learning to make
and hear confessions, they would find no refuge in religion. The
cross does not represent salvation; man's idea that suffering is re-
demptive is absurd. For Michaux, man's hope lies in his inner resistance to a life of crucifixion: "J'écris afin que ce qui était vrai ne

soit plus vrai. Prison montrée n'est plus prison" ("I write so that what was true will no longer be true. A prison revealed is no longer a prison," *P*, p. 146).

The drama of graphic writing which characterizes *Quatre Cents Hommes en croix* expresses Michaux's rage at the contradictory world of images: "Je n'ai rien à faire, je n'ai qu'à défaire" ("I have nothing to create, I only have to destroy," *E-R*, p. 35). Turning to plastic art, he releases his anger. With the death of his wife in 1947, beautifully expressed in the poignant *Nous Deux Encore* (*Still the Two of Us,* 1948), Michaux finds an innocence in the medium of painting, an innocence for him because of his lack of training. On the opening page of *Emergences-Résurgences,* he decries his verbal formation which entraps him in the absurdity of a world which extols and accepts suffering (crucifixion). Art becomes the outlet for his personal torment, as his slashes on paper represent the wounds inflicted by outer space; "Que de ce papier aussi vienne une plaie!" ("May a wound also come from this paper!" *E-R*, p. 36). Yet, these spontaneous outbursts are signs of his inner energy, power to create motion: "Signes revenus, pas les mêmes, plus du tout ce que je voulais faire et pas non plus en vue d'une langue — sortant tous du type homme, où jambes ou bras et buste peuvent manquer, mais homme par sa dynamique intérieure" ("Renewed signs, not the same, no longer at all what I wanted to do and not with a view to language either — all issuing from the human type, in which legs or arms and bust can be absent, but man through his inner dynamics," *E-R*, p. 50). The signs of *Mouvements* and *Par la voie des rythmes* reveal man's ability to survive. His very elasticity permits him to resist being crucified by outer space.

Thus, Michaux unstructures the hierarchy of the real through the force of energy: motion. Motion is the flow of potential dynamism and its very intensification negates form by reversing order and creating disorder. Dissembling the parts of the whole and obscuring attempts to identify forms expose an all-inclusive, non-ordered terrain of inner space. Destruction of the physical in the decomposed figures of *Mouvements* absolutizes speed ("Abstraction faite de VITESSE" — "SPEED apart," *FV*, p. 14), which is free from the dimensions of structure. As motion (energy, intensity, speed) is substituted for solidity, Michaux's esthetic universe overthrows the norms of language and vision; non-verbal signs replace words: *Par la voie des rythmes*. The reversal of order in *Quatre Cents Hommes en croix* first dislocates the suffering ordained by the real and then destroys the form (crucified) but not the force (energy) of expression (cross). Convergence of the real and the imagined occurs within when the reader discovers at the end of *La Vie dans les plis, Face au verrous,* and *Quatre Cents Hommes en croix* that he must return to the opening pages (*Liberté d'action, Mouvements,* and the title and first pages of *Quatre Cents Hommes en croix*). The actual arrangement of these volumes is not linear (linearity reflects the dimensions and directions of outer space), but circular (center). The experience of reading negates familiar literary approaches and destroys their limits (beginning, middle, end); decomposition of the parts releases an unfragmented whole. Michaux's revolt against all laws of composition and communication creates from within the multiform action-poem.

CHAPTER 7

The Vastness of Morpho-Creation

ARRÊTÉ par rien, tout existant partout (Stopped by nothing, everything coexisting everywhere, *MM,* p.181).

As early as his 1923 work, *Les Rêves et la jambe,* Michaux shows interest in the possibilities of drugs for the revelation of the psychic world. In *Ecuador* (1929), he admits to experimentation with ether and opium, but it is not until the first publication of *Misérable Miracle* in 1956[1] that he published texts and drawings conceived under the influence of drugs. His 1957 essay "Vitesse et tempo" ("Speed and Tempo")[2] explains his fascination with drug experimentation as morpho-creation: the examination of the actual processes of formation. Drugs so increase the speed of motor movement (signs) that the user is overcome by a vast amplification of his inner terrain and becomes capable of absorbing the sensory information of an ensemble: "Vastissime" ("The Tremendously Immense," *MM,* p. 178). Loss of the personality at an inhuman rate of speed results in the ecstatic feeling of unity, for the acceleration of tempo brings together inner and outer space: "Noyau d'énergie (c'est pourquoi son objet ou son origine n'importe) il est l'obstacle et le tremplin magique qui va me donner ma vitesse de libération" ("Core of energy [that's why its object or its origin doesn't matter] is the obstacle and the magic springboard which is going to give me my speed of liberation," *E-R,* p. 64).

Although Michaux's period of drug experimentation spans some sixteen years (1955-1971), the same period during which he notably writes less poetry and paints more, this is the one aspect of his work which has attracted the most attention. There are even attempts to situate him in the historical line of those French writers who have experimented with the writing of poetry while under the influence of drugs (Nerval, Baudelaire, Rimbaud, some Surrealists); yet

107

Michaux's drug texts hardly represent this tradition, for he approaches drugs as a scientist.[3] He is a clinician who is his own subject of objective study; the detached, controlled attitude which marks his works prior to 1956 remains the style of his drug texts. Moreover, all the prose works published during this period are arranged chronologically and are accompanied by retrospective commentaries and documentation. Ever objective in his approach to drugs, Michaux affirms that his writings and drawings are not those actually produced while under the influence of any given drug, but are, in fact, reconstructions. While this reflective quality of his drug works, regardless of form (prose, poetry, drawing) undermines their true psychedelic nature, these works do bring together two long-standing poles of human endeavor: science and art. Michaux as the artist-scientist attains a unity of expression by seeking knowledge of the psyche instead of an artificial paradise. In the miserable, turbulent gulfs of the drug world, he dislocates human sensibility and magnifies its insular operation. The miracle of infinity and peace lies in the discovery of the immensity of its absorption of the personality and in the revelation of its accessibility: "Séparé de la séparation / je vis dans un immense ensemble" ("Separated from separation / I live in an immense unity," *VC*, p. 26).

I   *Mescaline: Elation and Deflation*

While Michaux has explored the effects of marijuana, hemp, psilocybin, laudanum, ether, and L.S.D.,[4] one of two hallucinogenic poems, two of five prose studies, and most of his psychedelic drawings are related to his experiences with mescaline. These same works (written and plastic) cover the years 1955-1971 which mark his drug experimentation: *Misérable Miracle* (1956, 1972), *Paix dans les brisements* (*Peace in Debris*, 1957), and *L'Infini turbulent* (*The Turbulent Infinite*, 1957, 1964). In these texts, Michaux both extols the liberation from the finite produced by mescaline and rejects it as a mutation of independent psychic space. Despite these two opposing attitudes, the texts reveal a vastness of unity, a plenitude of being; this is unequaled in his prior works.

Misérable Miracle, L'Infini turbulent, and the 1968-1971 Addenda to *Misérable Miracle* are a trilogy of the mescaline experience. In fact, Michaux terms *Misérable Miracle* as the first series of experiments, the commentaries of *L'Infini turbulent* as the second series (and it is to this series that *Paix dans les brisements* belongs), while the Addenda form the conclusion to both series. The first series is announced in the 1955 introduction to *Misérable Miracle* as an exploration: "Par les mots, les signes, les dessins, la Mescaline est l'explorée" ("Through words, signs, sketches, Mescaline is the explored," *MM*, p. 13). The experience is one of optical changes, visions, distortions, contradictory desires and feelings; it ruins lines by breaking up inner terrain: "Liée au verbal, elle rédige par énumération. Liée à l'espace et à la figuration, elle dessine par répétition. Et par symétrie (symétrie sur symétrie)" ("Linked to the verbal, it writes by enumeration. Linked to space and to figuration, it sketches by repetition. And by symmetry [symmetry upon symmetry]," *MM*, p. 65). The undulating products of the mescaline drama are such a model of symmetry that the resulting work is "un mécanisme d'infinité" ("A mechanism of infinity," *MM*, p. 76), which can go on and on, but which still partakes of spatial dimensions and directions, the *plis*: "On me remuait, on me faisait faire des plis" ("I was being stirred, I was made to make folds," *MM*, p. 15).

In the fourth chapter of *Misérable Miracle,* Michaux discusses hashish as a point of comparison with the hallucinogenic mescaline, but the sketches attempted under the influence of hashish are more incomplete than the endless visionary mescaline sketches ("Le Haschich ne fait pas que des tableaux. Il commet des actes" — "Hashish doesn't just make pictures. It commits acts," *MM*, p. 108). Rejecting hashish because it actively accepts problems instead of resolving them, Michaux takes a larger dose of mescaline (Chapter 5), only to experience uncontrolled furor and fears, madness in perverse impulses, obsession with pursuing false ideas (*MM*, p. 143), and the destruction of all judgment. Self-control is slowly regained, and, in the return of his will, Michaux finds value in the interruptions of his psychic space caused by mescaline: "La santé de l'esprit consisterait au contraire à rester maître de sa vitesse" ("On the contrary, health of the mind would consist of remaining master of its speed," *MM*, p. 164). Consequently, the frontispiece to the 1972 edition is a drawing of the chemical symbol which signals proprietorship over the work at hand: "Pourquoi avoir cessé de prendre de la Mescaline? Pas fiable. Pas maniable comme on le voudrait" ("Why did I stop taking Mescaline? Unreliable. Not so easy to handle as one would like it to be," *MM*, p. 195).

As the first series of mescaline experiences reveal the schizophrenic effects of the experience, the interruptions, the second series concentrates on the extreme psychic vibrations induced by the drug. *L'Infini turbulent* begins with a discussion of the effects of mescaline, then relates eight experiments, and ends with a comparison to other hallucinogenics (hemp, hashish, L.S.D.). The 1964 edition adds a final discussion of drugs and erotic behavior.

Michaux finds that superlatives are necessary for any discussion of the extremism of the vibrating images which mescaline unleashes: "Mescaline accélératrice, répétitive, agitatrice, accentuatrice, renverseuse de toute rêverie, interruptrice. Démonstrance du discontinu" ("Mescaline is accelerative, repetitive, agitating, accentuator, overthrower of all reverie, interruptor. Demonstration of the discontinuous," *IT*, p. 12). While the experience of *Misérable Miracle* is the discovery of the turbulence wrought by mescaline, *L'Infini turbulent* is a more analytical work than its predecessor, if not a more objective one. While Michaux does not hesitate to express his interior visions, be they ecstatic or nightmarish, he remains detached and clinical — so much so that the artist is almost lost from view. Throughout *L'Infini turbulent*, there are only infrequent moments of jubilation: "L'infini peut être abordé selon trois modes, selon le mode pur, selon le mode diabolique, selon le mode démentiel" ("The infinite can be approached in three ways, on a pure level, a diabolic level, a demented level," *IT*, p. 21). Nevertheless, the infinite is there, confirmed as existing and affirmed as within the realm of human experience ("l'infini est là," *IT*, p. 199).

The eight experiments of *L'Infini turbulent* progress from joy to disillusionment. In the first five, Michaux expresses a sensation of assimilation; all awareness of order (physical, mental) disappears into a poem of absolute purity: "L'extase, c'est coopérer à la divine création du monde" ("Ecstasy is cooperating in the divine creation of the world," *IT*, p. 79). The loss of bodily and psychological differentiation results in complete detachment of the personality from all indicators of identity. The elation in dissolution ("La jouissance de la déliquescence," *IT*, p. 100) is a going beyond of choice, preference, and decision: "Je ne suis dans la mescaline que pour la surnature" ("I am into mescaline only for the extraordinary," *IT*, p. 128). But, in the midst of this deliquescence is a new discovery: mescaline is untrustworthy, for each experience is different:

"Drogue traîtresse" ("Treacherous drug," *IT*, p. 113). Michaux rejects his efforts to draw because of the mechanistic qualities of his sketches: "La mescaline ne fait jamais nature. Elle ne connaît pas ça. Elle est compositeur et mécanicienne. . . Mais c'est créer que je veux" ("Mescaline never follows nature. It doesn't know that. It is a compositor and a mechanic. . . But what I want is to create," *IT*, p. 139).

In comparing mescaline to other hallucinogenic drugs, hemp, hashish, and L.S.D. in "Domaine mescalinien et domaines voisins" ("Mescaline Domain and Neighboring Domains") and in "L.S.D. 25," Michaux finds that drugs actually bring about duality. Hemp constrains, hashish accentuates, and L.S.D. produces a frenzy which borders on the loss of all initiative: "Jamais on n'est plus sûr de la réalité que lorsqu'elle est illusion. Car elle est réalité alors par adhésion" ("You can never be surer of reality than when it is illusion. For it is then reality by adherence," *IT*, p. 156). Mescaline alone permits the experience of a supraterrestrial world, but in the ecstasy is extreme agitation at the loss of all sense of orientation and self-control.

The essay "Le Problème d'Eros dans les drogues hallucinogènes" ("The Problem of Eros in Hallucinogenic Drugs"), which was added to the 1964 edition of *L'Infini turbulent*, confirms the release of hostilities and fears, as well as deviations from accord: "Peyotl et mescaline, il faut le répéter, ne valent vraiment que par la transe" ("The only real value of peyote and mescaline, it bears repeating, is in the trance," *IT*, p. 211). Drugs rarely induce erotic love; their electrical purgation of the ego tends rather to generate a feeling of compassion and the illusion of contact with the Absolute (*IT*, p. 231).

While *Misérable Miracle* and *L'Infini turbulent* tend to emphasize the devastation of the psyche which drug usage causes, to the point that these works can be labeled texts of deflation, the moments of elation are the subject of *Paix dans les brisements (Peace in Debris*, 1959), a mescaline poem which is accompanied by thirteen sketches. In two short introductions to the free verse poem "Signification des dessins" ("Meaning of the Drawings") and "Au sujet de *Paix dans les brisements*" ("About *Peace in Debris*"),[5] Michaux reflects on the fragmented paroxysms of his mescaline experiences and finds in their redistribution an experience of unity. While *Misérable Miracle* and *L'Infini turbulent* are characterized by negative statements and key terms of rupture, indicated by the prefix *dé-* *(dégringolade—tumble)*, *Paix dans les brisements* is a text dominated by terms of reassembly which are marked by affirmative construction and the prefix *re-* *(reconstituer — reconstitute)*: "Le poème mille foix brisé pèse et pousse pour se constituer, pour un immense jour mémorable reconstituer, pour, à travers tout, nous reconstituer" ("Broken up a thousand times, the poem presses and strives to establish itself, for one immense memorable day to reconstitute, through everything, to reconstitute us," *PB*, p. 33). Even the sketches are described as reconstitutions, not only reworkings of drawings, but also evocations of the freedom of the psyche to attain the pure: "Je crois montrer un phénomène de base . . . éclatant et nu . . . qui . . . est primitif et général" ("I believe that I am showing a basic phenomenon . . . brilliant and bare . . . which . . . is . . . primitive and general," *PB*, pp. 30-31).

The title of the poem expresses this very fusion of the fragments ("brisements") into an effortless vision and sensation of harmonious unity: "paix." Peace in this text refers to the absence of the need to intervene; the hostile situation is literally so disorganized that its pieces no longer affect the personality. Thoughts cease to be governed by the need to resist obstacles, for there are no folds or bolts. While the vocabulary is based on a pattern of words which reflect upward movement (*ascension*) and those which express downward motion (*pente*), *Paix dans les brisements* is topographically a rendering of the debris which forms a composite whole. As the poet descends further and further into the depths of his being and the resulting flotsam of his dislocated situation whirls downward on the page, the eye is constantly made to race to the top of the next page because of the use of the technique of inversion, for to fall is to rise — literally and figuratively: "la pente vers le haut" ("sloping down towards the top," *PB*, p. 47). Similarly, the drawings move downward, then upward until they go off the page. The technical use of short and long sentences and attention to spacing on the page generate in the reader the desire for union. The reader is so overwhelmed by the constant barrage of the signs of rupture before him that he spontaneously reacts against the crumbling sentences and words ("tchit," "pf," "dipht," "j...") in a search for a base of organization, as well as relief (peace) from the onslaught. Whether the words are real words or unrecognizable distortions of words, the reader responds to the vibrations of the visually verbal fragments and is caught up in the rhythm of the repeated terms which create an echo effect. Significantly, the one term which is reiterated more than any other is *infini (infinity),* and its recurrence, like the hammering of words in *Epreuves, exorcismes,* gives rise to the demand for reconstitution. It is interesting to note that the words of the title do not appear in the text; the text is the crumbling disequilibrium, while the end, expressed in a long phrase of soft sounds, brings the desired tranquility: "la merveilleuse simple inarrêtable ascension" ("the marvelous simple unstoppable ascension," *PB,* p. 47). The turbulence of the reading experience gives way to the infinite.

II *Demystification and Delusion*

In *Connaissance par les gouffres* (*Learning through Despair,* 1961), Michaux undertakes a study of the effects of drugs on human sensibility and on the ability to function mentally. The discovery that drugs radically affect motor movement and alter the senses in *Misérable Miracle* and *L'Infini turbulent* is now followed by a rather painstaking exploration of the transformative power of drugs in an attempt to gain knowledge of the human psyche and how it actually operates. In the first chapter, "Comment agissent les drogues?" ("How Do Drugs Operate?"), Michaux discusses the paradox of his experiments and studies to date. Drug experiences alternate between a succession of visions and feelings of the presence of the infinite and the magnification of the sensation of separation. The dual qualities of the vision and impulses induced by drugs exist without any refinement of intellectual judgment at the time of their occurrence; squares become triangles, but this transformation is not recognized as a disorientation of the psyche until the end. Yet this metamorphosis of basic forms does point to the possible existence of a third state, one in which there is neither alternation, nor antagonism: "Univers pur, d'une totale homogénéité énergétique où vit ensemble, et en flots, l'absolument de même race, de même signe, de même orientation" ("A pure universe, with a completely energetic homogeneity where the absolute in identical race, identical sign, identical orientation dwell together, and in great quantity," *CG,* p. 32). Hence, the remaining five sections of *Connaissance par les gouffres* are dedicated to the revelation of a universe demystified of mental laws, where squares and triangles are the same and one is not even aware of their metamorphosis.

In "La Psilocybine," Michaux becomes the self-critic of his 1958 experiences with the psychotoxic drug, psilocybin. Psilocybin depersonalizes because it affects muscular movement; all physical strength is sapped at the same time as mobilization is suppressed. The derealization of any sense of adventure creates a passivity which is the experience of separatism: "Je n'avais plus mon style. Mon style avait perdu ses 'soudains' " ("I no longer had my style. My style had lost its 'surprises,' " *CG,* p. 66). The feelings of anti-independence and anti-singularity — the loss of style — which occur under psilocybin do not alleviate antagonism.

In Chapter 3, "La Mescaline et la musique," Michaux reports finding that all words and tones are the same. The experience of the abstract denies the experience of listening to the music itself. Understanding comes afterward, but at the moment of hearing the music, he discovers such distortions of the words, the tones, even the meaning that there is actually no experience of the music at all.

The fourth section, "Cannabis indica," is devoted to "neotenic" thought, thought which is incomplete, as stimulated by hashish. The words remain half-born and most of them have been felt and seen before. While he has a sense of modulation — exchanges between terms and even pleasant daydreams — there is very little loss of the personality under the influence of hashish, and the sense of succession remains. Alternation is not overcome by hashish, although it is viewed by Michaux as the most manageable of the drugs.

"Situations-gouffres" ("Abysmal-Situations") forms the largest part of *Connaissance par les gouffres.* Twelve problems and difficulties caused by feelings of alienation are scrutinized in an effort to study another kind of mental functioning, that of the alienated being, "pour surprendre des mystères ailleurs cachés" ("in order to uncover the mysteries hidden elsewhere," *CG*, p. 179). The traps which drug usage creates are many: loss of objective value, loss of any sense of presence, chaos, disorientation in the situation, a babel of sensations, impotence with regard to decision-making, delirium which leads to megalomania, inadaptability which approaches the catatonic, withdrawal when all contact is obliterated. These pitfalls ("situations-gouffres") destroy the psyche and foster acute alienation rather than integration. The same disillusioning discovery occurs in the final chapter, "Au sujet des dissociations et de la conscience seconde" ("About Disassociations and the Second Conscience"). The pluripersonalization which drugs induce takes the form of such violent feelings of disconnection that hysteria and mythomania result. The subconscious remains unsatisfied in its aspiration for unity.

The knowledge gleaned from the studies and experiments in *Connaissance par les gouffres* demystifies drugs as a means of attaining a paradisiacal ecstasy. The totality of the psyche is fragmented; its visions of a compassionate, harmonious universe are annihilated by magnified sensations of ruin, devastation, and alienation. Redistribution of human sensibility releases more problems than it solves. The third state of no alternation between succession and separation, possession and dispossession, remains elusive, although aspiration for this state is intact.

The obstacles encountered in the search for the unlimited experience of harmony is the subject of the seven parts of *Vents et poussières* (*Winds and Dust*, 1962), which spans the seven years of experiments set forth in *Misérable Miracle, L'Infini turbulent, Paix dans les brisements,* and *Connaissance par les gouffres,* 1955-1962. In the eight prose sections of the first part, "Vents et poussières," Louana, a fictive character, tires of her miserable life and seeks a catalyst which will project her out of her tragic situation. Desiring the intangible, she finds only obstacles: "Le vent et la poussière me poussent vers la mer" ("Wind and dust push me toward the sea," *VEP*, p. 10). Failure to attain the unattainable is continued in "Le Voyage difficile" ("The Difficult Voyage"), where a people made of dust conflict with the hard form of a stone which has been assumed by the poet; yet the dust people are ineffective against this inhuman form, and he continues the difficult trip, seeking a breath of air, life ("Le souffle, où était le souffle?" *VEP*, p. 21). The notion of a laborious journey continues in "Vacances" ("Vacation"); no matter where the traveler goes, he encounters contradictions, a lack of understanding, and finally disinterest in any change of scene.

The futility of the first three parts of *Vents et poussières* is overcome in the fourth section, "Leurs Secrets en spectacle" ("Their Secrets on Show"), in which Michaux examines drawings made by those with mental problems: "Devant leurs tableaux d'abord je rêvais. . . ; traversant le réel, dont il défait l'importance'' ("In front of their pictures I would first dream. . . ; crossing the real, whose importance is destroyed," *VEP*, p. 33). The outer space frustration of "Vents et poussières," "Le Voyage difficile," and "Vacances" are more disillusioning than the drawings by insane people. In "Iniji,"[6] Michaux returns to inner terrain, as he exorcizes the qualities of weight and oppression in an incantation to Iniji, the Islamic spirit who possesses such supernatural powers as the ability to make air visible. The three mescaline drawings which accompany "Iniji" consist of fluid repetitive lines which mirror the poet's physical desire to break the cocoon of physical existence. The threads of words which bind in "Iniji" are broken in "Cahiers d'Orga, signés Orga" ("Orga's Notebooks, Signed Orga"). The Orga plan is to provoke expression; forcing a break-up of language renews it: "Tout, véritablement tout est à recommencer par la base: par les cellules, de plantes, de moines, de proto-animaux: l'alphabet de la vie" ("Everything, truly everything is to be done again from the bottom: cells, plants, monks, proto-animals: the alphabet of life," *VEP*, p. 70). The one drawing which illustrates "Cahiers d'Orga, signés Orga" differs from Michaux's usual mescaline sketches in that the small tight lines take the form of a headless body and capture the complex network of inner motion.

In the conclusion to *Vents et poussières,* "Le Champ de ma conscience" ("The Field of My Conscience"), Michaux takes up the incessant energy which characterizes the human psyche: "Dans le champ de ma conscience, il n'y a pas de fixité" ("In the field of my conscience, there is no fixity," *VEP*, p. 77). The rapid appearance-disappearance of feelings and visions renews the subjective world: "A la porte de ma conscience . . . des massacres . . ., des fêtes . . ., des combats, des exaltations" ("On the threshold of my conscience . . . massacres. . . , celebrations. . . , battles, exaltations," *VEP*, p. 81). Motion — wind — and whatever it stirs up — dust — testify to the reality and dynamism of inner space.

Alienation, then, is an important sign of integration. Experience of the abnormal permits knowledge of the normal, and impotency of action gives birth to the desire for the strength to move. The ultimate value of the years of drug experimentation is their production of evidence that the psyche exists in a continuum of images: "Je reçevais . . . la preuve que l'image est un certain immédiat que le langage ne peut traduire que de très loin, et qu'elle a dans l'esprit une place vraiment à part, matière première pour la pensée" ("I obtained proof that the image is a certain immediacy which language can only translate imperfectly and that it has in the psyche a place truly apart, raw material for thought," *E-R*, p. 84).

Confirmation that the psyche in operation creates thought and fashions its own images is found in Michaux's last prose study of the alienating effects of drugs, *Les Grandes Epreuves de l'esprit et les innombrables petites* (*Great Trials of the Mind and Countless Minor Ones,* 1966) and in its companion text on freedom from limits, *Vers la complétude* (*Towards Fulfillment,* 1967). *Les Grandes Epreuves de l'esprit et les innombrables petites* begins with an analysis of "Le Merveilleux Normal" ("The Normal Marvelous"). Disorientation through drugs reveals the abnormal inability to know how to think and its opposite: "Je voudrais dévoiler les mécanismes complexes, qui font de l'homme avant tout un opérateur" ("I would like to reveal the complex mechanisms which make man first of all an operator," *GE*, p. 9). The return to the self after the drug experience in "Revenir à soi, qu'est-ce que c'est?" ("To Come To, What Is It?") brings with it a reorganization of the power to think: "Car penser . . . c'est . . . placer les éléments dans le champ pensant, c'est savoir mettre le cap sur l'acquis" ("For thinking . . . is . . . placing elements in the thinking arena, is knowing how to head for experience," *GE*, pp. 17-18). The repetition of visions, words, and images is, in the long run, a form of moderation which alters the succession of thoughts and proposes a counter-tension to the authority of the real; the two opposing tensions neutralize each other. Hence, Michaux's examination of the repetitive alternating quality of the drug experience affirms his earlier theory and practice of counterbalance for the establishment of an equilibrium.

Ordinarily, the elasticity of the conscience creates a continuum which makes an image, but the difficulty of maintaining the operation of the thought processes in "En difficulté mais où la difficulté?" ("In Trouble, But Where is the Trouble?") can be thwarted by the unnatural state of drowsiness, which is a soporific to life and curbs its fluidity. Other impediments to image-making include too much speed, which decomposes and never recomposes, and tranquillizers, such as librium, which make action impossible and create false situations. Any multiplication of occurrences is defined as alienation which hampers thought (Part III). Things which should not be present (in "Les présences qui ne devraient pas être là") are those interruptions (noises, vertigo), which prevent the retention of visions and ideas. While the use of "c.i.," one of the oldest substances which induces psychic shock, simplifies matter to such a degree that there is no feeling of earth, only a sensation of expansion, there are no words for the expression of infinite space ("Le Dépouillement par l'espace"—"Spoliation through Space").

The sixth section, "Conscience de soi ravagée" ("Ravaged Self-Consciousness"), concerns Michaux's study of freedom from corporeal limits, immateriality. The absence of sensation can lead to two extreme mental abnormalities. First, hypochondria, a narcissism of the body, can occur because of the measure of confidence which refuses to accept the loss of a part of the body and demands a redoubled effort to know that it is there. The situation changes for the hypochondriac, but it remains a situation. Second, schizophrenia can result because of the exasperation felt by total atomization of the body. There are no frontiers of the self to be defended, much less identified, and all possibility of a convergence of the parts is viewed as non-existent. The problem of multiplicity in "Le Besoin de surcharger et de désimplifier" ("The Need To Overload and To Complicate") becomes the normal, since discord is, at least, a measure of self-control, while the experience of the singular (loss of sensation and its subsequent loss of differentiation) leads to extreme frustration. The eleven sequences of studies in "Aliénations expérimentales" ("Experimental Alienations") span a range of abnormal experiences: physical ephemeralness, loss of self-mastery, being a free spirit with no material attachments, loss of psychic domain, being surrounded by hostile objects, mental fixations and obsessions, agitation at the inability to make definitions and identifications.

In the concluding commentary of these eleven experiments, Michaux finds that he has been in error to attempt to show the intelligible aspects of abnormal psychic behavior (*GE*, p. 179). Rather, the break with associations of outer space and the elimination of their interrelationships should be seen as a renewal of the inner self, and this notion is continued in the two final sections, "Les Quatre Mondes" ("The Four Worlds") and "Commentaires." The inexplicability of the immensity of psychic space is accepted now as a total gift of the self to the fluvial feeling of accord, love. The normal state of being often confuses what is good and bad for an individual because it is characterized by distractions and plurality, the profane. In contrast, the abnormal gives clear distinctions through its dislocation of the profane; removal of the habitual and the familiar opens up the vastness of the creative power of psychic energy. The negative experiences of the abnormal state are inverted into the joy of going beyond duality: "Félicité par dépersonnalisation" ("Felicity through depersonalization," *GE*, p. 203). Energetic absorption of the self leads to the absolute, a plenitude of being: "L'absolu: la vraie non-violence" ("The absolute: true non-violence," *GE*, p. 204).

Hence, in *Les Grandes Epreuves de l'esprit et les innombrables petites,* Michaux reveals that the conscience can participate in an ensemble because it is capable of creation (revealing things which have no other existence): "Lorsqu'il y a apparition, le rapport avec la figure apparaissante, la participation accapare. . . On fait partie d'un ensemble. Cette conscience occupe" ("When there is appearance, relationship with the appearing figure, participation is secured. . . . One is part of a whole. This awareness keeps one busy," *GE*, p. 170, n. 2).

Access to the spacious infinite of the fullness of being becomes the structure and theme of *Vers la complétude* (*Toward Fulfillment*, 1967), but the vocabulary which characterizes this text of limitlessness is that of *Les Grandes Epreuves de l'esprit et les innombrables petites* and depends upon it for a full understanding of the terms. Written in fragments similar to *Paix dans les brisements* and relying on repetition of words and phrases to echo oneness, *Vers la complétude* is a hymn to unity: "Par dessus tout / effaçant tout / Unité" ("Beyond everything / effacing everything / Unity," *VC*, p. 24). Alienation from the limits of both physical and customary psychological space through vibrations which are in accord with the vastness of limitlessness obliterates feelings of dislocation and disorientation: "L'édifice plie" ("The structure bends," *VC*, p. 15; that is, outer space caves in). Destruction of the multiple normal creates plenitude: "Rien / seulement Rien / 'Rien' s'élève du naufrage" ("Nothing / only Nothing / 'Nothing' rises from the shipwreck," *VC*, p. 23). Nothing is the unformed All: "Un lieu est donné / quand tous les lieux sont retirés" ("A place is granted / when all places are withdrawn," *VC*, p. 27). As Michaux's subtitle for *Vers la complétude* indicates, the actual seizure of the experience of unity is the release of outer space forms: "Saisie et Dessaisies" ("Seizure and Releases").

Michaux's passage from the world of signs to the universe of induced agitation is marked, indeed, by the revelation of the experience of unity. His analyses in prose, free verse, and drawings of what happens under the influence of drugs do testify to the existence and nature of the psyche and unveil psychological space. But Michaux is also critical of his drug experiences, and he finally rejects the use of drugs as an unnatural means by which to gain access to the fullness of being. Hence, many of the titles of his works on drug experimentation are contradictions: *Misérable Miracle, L'Infini turbulent, Paix dans les brisements, Vents et poussières, Connaissance par les gouffres.* Only two works written during these years bear integrated titles, *Les Grandes Epreuves de l'esprit et les innombrables petites* and *Vers la complétude,* although neither is truly complete, for the first title suggests that there may be some conflicting evidence and the second one indicates a direction only, *vers,* not an arrival. Even Michaux's psychedelic drawings, his "dessins mescaliniens" and "dessins de réagrégation," show multiplication and plurality, rather than unity.

Drugs reveal the existence of psychic unity, but they do not create it: "La drogue . . . est plus révélatrice que créatrice" ("Drugs . . . are more revelatory than creative," *GE,* p. 33). In the 1968-1971 Addenda to the 1972 edition of *Misérable Miracle,* Michaux praises drugs for having opened to him the aspatial and atemporal Absolute, the end of the finite, but drugs remain an opening and an opening only to the Infinite. The obstacle in drugs lies in their creation of a dependency problem, which renders self-control impossible: "Mettons que je ne suis pas très doué pour la dépendence" ("Let's say that I am not really gifted for dependency," *MM,* p. 195). Consequently, Michaux's discovery during the drug years is the personal experience of actual participation in the vastness of the psyche, demonstrated in his morpho-creations; but these years represent only one of his passages to the creation of unity: "Sans intermédiaire la participation au divin aussitôt est offerte à chacun" ("Without an intermediary, participation in the divine is immediately offered to everyone," *MM,* p. 184). For Michaux, the expression of fusion is not enough; the artistic adventure must also include the creation of natural access to the unity of inner and outer space.

CHAPTER 8

The Design of Destiny

Principe sans discours,
Principe de tout principe
Retour au Principe
(Principle without discourse,
Principle of every principle
Return to the Principle, *MO*, p. 129).

WHILE Henri Michaux's drug experiments affirm the capacity of the human psyche to expand and participate in an Absolute, his written and sketched works during these years do not fully capture the feeling of vibratory unity which the drug experiences make possible. Unlike film, pen and ink sketches are a fixed medium which may indicate movement but do not in themselves move. In fact, Michaux's drug works are the results of the chaos which emerges from the destruction of outer space referentials. In a re-examination of his "dessins de désagrégation" in *Emergences-Résurgences* (1972), Michaux finds that the tortuous lines fall short of capturing the actual sensation of a peace which is beyond intervention, beyond the lines themselves. Struck by the very symmetry of his psychedelic drawings, Michaux discovers the mandala, an immutable homeostatic vision in which linear fragmentation and dispersal are actually reflective of coherence; that is, the immobility of the pen and ink works is evidence of a counter-life: "Résumé graphique d'une situation d'ensemble, de la plus métaphysique. Peinture par oubli de soi, et de ce qu'on voit ou qu'on pourrait voir, peinture de ce qu'on sait, expression de sa place dans le Monde" ("A graphic résumé of a comprehensive situation, of a most metaphysical one. Painting through forgetfulness of self, and of what one sees or one might see, painting of what one knows, ex-

121

pression of one's place in the World," *E-R*, pp. 102-103).

The graphic squaring of the circle which the mandala represents replaces aggression by contemplation. As the circle of unity and the square of multiplicity lose their separate identies and relationships, the visual synthesis of the mandala goes beyond all referentials, including the distinction between inner and outer space. Concentration on the constant division of the parts so obscures the parts themselves that only a harmonious whole remains. Michaux's disruptive lines negate each other and all measurable qualities; going in all directions at once, they lose all considerations of space and time. Visual and verbal dispersal are, then, artistic evidence of synthesis and ultimate order: "Calme du fondamental. Retour à la base. L'Inutile enfin dissipé" ("Calm of the fundamental. Return to foundations. The Useless is finally done away with," *FSD*, p. 177). The absolute sovereignty of the human psyche in its ability to gain access to the pure substance of life — the formless All — is manifested in the compact, but all-inclusive mandala, as Michaux's "yantra" (tool) takes up all square and round-shaped forms and levels them into the indivisible whole, which is known by its whole and not by its parts: "Force sans face / Matrice des formes et rempart contre les formes" ("Faceless Force / Matrix of forms and bulwark against forms," *MO*, p. 126). As flux gives way to synthesis, Michaux's work for the past several years has begun to unveil the privileged moments of unity: *Façons d'endormi, façons d'éveillé (Sleeping Modes, Waking Modes,* 1969), *Poteaux d'angle (Corner Posts,* 1971), *Emergences-Résurgences* (1972), *Moments: Traversées du temps (Moments: Passages of Time,* 1973), and *Face à ce qui se dérobe (Facing What is Disappearing,* 1975).

I *The Rhythm of Reverie*

One of the frustrating aspects of Michaux's years of drug experimentation is his recognition of a dependency factor. Even years later, he is not free from the effects of drugs: "Après des années, sans prendre aucune substance hallucinogène, il reste un appel à la fragmentation" ("Years later, without taking any hallucinogenic substance, a call to fragmentation remains," *E-R*, p. 106). Access to a glimpse of the Absolute is tarnished by the need for an external stimulant, which reduces self-mastery. Yet effective dispersal of self-consciousness under the influence of drugs does reveal a dynamic inner space which counteracts external situations. Cognizant of man's history of fascination with dreams as a means of transforming his relationship with the world, Michaux undertakes an exploration of dreams as a possible terrain for responding to outer space exigencies. Written with the same detached scientific style which characterizes his drug texts, Michaux's dream studies in *Façons d'endormi, façons d'éveillé* (*Sleeping Modes, Waking Modes*) offer a dispassionate analysis of the various categories of dreams. But, unlike his drug texts, the opening pages of this work are marked by skepticism as to the subject matter at hand. Admitting his own reluctance to relate and explain his dreams, Michaux confesses that it is the optical quality of the dream experience that leads him to undertake such an examination. In other words, Michaux informs his reader quickly and from the outset that there are no possible affinities with the Surrealist attitude towards dreams.

Divided into two major sections, *Façons d'endormi, façons d'éveillé* is based on the formal distinction between dream (*rêve*) and daydreaming (*rêverie*), between the images that occur while one is asleep (*endormi*) and those visionary products which are created by the imagination while one is awake (*éveillé*). The first and longer section is devoted to a careful analysis of dreams and is marked by a clinical approach to the subject. In contrast, the shorter section on reverie is less dispassionate and more poetic. Michaux's treatment of *rêve* is, then, stylistically closer to his drug studies, while his explorations of *rêverie* are more akin to the prose style of *Passages*; hence, dreams are imitative and reflect subservience, while reverie is creative and affirms freedom: "Le contraire du rêve . . . la rêverie, dispose de liberté. Elle demande à en avoir. Elle en fait sa jouissance" ("The opposite of the dream . . . reverie, has freedom at its command. It insists on having it. It is its delight," *FE*, p. 197).

Divided into five parts, the section on dreams is an attempt to observe accurately the emotions and images which come about during the state of sleep. In "Rideau des rêves" ("Curtain of Dreams"), Michaux finds a problem of unity between the experience itself and its presentation which, perforce, must come after the experience. The very incongruities which abound in the nature of dream study (recall, reflection) lead him first to dismiss dream recitation ("récit de rêve") as a possible approach and second to the discovery that all his dreams are based on his personal experiences and are not in themselves new experiences. For Michaux, the dream world is dependent upon the affective memory of the dreamer: "Le rêve reprend ces éléments, en somme tous performés déjà" ("The dream revives these elements, all of which, when all is said and done, have already been performed," *FE*, p. 35). While dreams may be revelatory, they do not offer any new discoveries, a conclusion already drawn from the drug experiences. "Tempérament de nuit" ("Nocturnal Mood") reinforces Michaux's failure to discern any creative possibility in dreams: the images tend to be prosaic because they are directly related to regular images in his own life. On the other hand, he is struck by the magical rhythm which characterizes daydreams ("rêves d'éveillé") and, in contrast, reinforces the mediocrity of his dreams and their lack of movement.

Dreams reflect the ordinary events of daily life. While they may change the order of the events and even confuse them, they remain part of the order of the material real world.

In "Quelques Rêves, quelques remarques" ("A Few Dreams, A Few Remarks"), Michaux relates eight dreams and then gives commentary on each one. He discovers that the dream only denatures the real; it does not really change it. The following part, "Transformations," reverses the procedure: he lists first the facts of the event and then describes the dream. In the final part on dreams, "Reflexions," Michaux concludes that, while dreams are responses that react against the discipline of outer space, they represent just another system, that is, a disorder or inversion of the real. The only value which Michaux is willing to assign to the dream experience is its role in helping the dreamer understand better his awakened state. Because the dream cannot be divorced from the dreamer's external situation, it remains an expression of outer space: "Mais tout rêve, si peu spectaculaire qu'il soit, est asservissement" ("But every dream, no matter how unspectacular it may be, is a subservience," *FE*, p. 192).

The note of disappointment which marks Michaux's discoveries of dependency, stasis, imitation of the real, and substitution of one system for another in his study of dreams in the first major section of *Façons d'endormi, façons d'éveillé* is replaced in the second section by a tone of excitement. In fact, throughout "Les Rêves vigiles" ("Vigilant Dreams"), Michaux's style reflects a joyful mood. Writing literally in an atmosphere of confidence in the exploration of daydreams, his expression is so much more forceful and enthusiastic that the tones alone contrast the merits of reverie with those of dream: *"Un champ de forces, voilà le rêve vigile"* (*"A field of energy, that's the vigilant dream," FE*, p. 202).

Dream (*rêve*) is passive, repetitious of experience in outer space, and mediocre in quality, while reverie is active and unlimited in its possibilities: "Rêverie, art pur. Le seul. Et pour soi seul" ("Reverie, pure art. The only one. And for it alone,"*FE*, p. 201). Because daydreaming is a dynamic activity, it is synonymous with absolute personal freedom: "Là où était l'écrasement, je fais, j'ai le dépassement; là où était le dégoût, je fais, j'ai l'émerveillement; là où j'étais devenu petit, je fais, j'ai la grandeur; là où l'on me tenait, je crée, j'ai la souveraineté" ("Where there was prostration, I act, I have transcendence; where there was weariness, I act, I have admiration; where I had become insignificant, I act, I have importance; where I was held, I create, I have sovereignty," *FE*, p. 237). Reverie alone is all-inclusive and non-exclusive; unlike dream, it has no definable limits, nor does it have qualities which can be subjected to discipline or systematization. Reverie includes the violent and the peaceful, flux and immobility, the familiar and the unknown. Generically free from affective memory and experience, the fluidity of reverie emerges as Michaux's creative rhythm, which, by its expression of inner energy, can change any object and open new dimensions to experience.

In his study of René Magritte's paintings, *En rêvant à partir de peintures énigmatiques* (*On Dreaming Starting With Enigmatic Paintings,* 1972), Michaux finds that Magritte's reverie, as expressed by his work, serves as a source of meditation for his own reverie. It does not matter if Magritte's work seems to falsify nature; it matters only that in his painting he gives the impression of reigning over nature and outer space in general. Value becomes a devaluation; for the refusal to reflect a generally held hierarchy of meaning is exactly what stimulates the spectator and leads him into new musings or reveries of his own. Written originally in 1964, before he actually met Magritte, Michaux finds an inner freedom of thoughts and images not previously experienced; his approach to paintings by another artist remains his own. Once he has come to know Magritte the person, however, his previous freedom of access to the plastic visions is limited by the outer space situation which imposes a personality onto the vision.

Knowing Magritte brings to bear on Michaux's optical base a combination of the man and the artist; signposts of definition and knowledge infringe on the voyage of the imagination. In his group of aphorisms, *Poteaux d'angle (Corner Posts,* 1971), Michaux reaffirms the disordering attitude of inadaptation: "Non, non, pas acquérir. Voyage pour t'appauvrir" ("No, no, not for acquisition. Travel in order to impoverish yourself," *PA*, p. 10). Knowledge and experiences of outer space (such as his meeting Magritte the man) construct referentials, and compose systems of order. The acquisition of facts, figures, forms reflects the oppressiveness of the material world and leads to acquiescence. In opposition to the system of referentials posed by outer space confrontation, Michaux continues to place in motion all attributes, qualities, activities, even the practicalities, that serve to particularize objects and reaffirm multiplicity. His attacks on the relationships of things to each other and on their measurable considerations in terms of time and space are reflected in the expression of continuous expansion: "Je veux plutôt un monde potentiel que réel" ("I prefer a potential world to a real one," *FE*, p. 220). Consequently, the potential existence which Magritte's vision projects replaces analysis by synthesis. It is only in knowing Magritte that Michaux finds that he begins to seek the particular components in the painting before him, rather than responding to their harmonious unity.

In the collected volume, *Moments: Traversées du temps* (*Moments: Passages of Time,* 1973), Michaux unveils the all-inclusive adventure of flux as a process of concentrating on the division of the parts to such an extent that all awareness of separateness disappears. Where *L'Espace du dedans* and *Passages* reflect his verbal dislocation of the spatial real, *Moments* crystallizes his temporal demobilization of points in time as well as points in space. In a formal sense, the very unity of *Moments* lies in its disunity. Its eleven sections are drawn from such a broad range of Michaux's explorations that their actual arrangement in the volume dislocates and destroys their original contextual identities. By his placement of texts in *Moments,* Michaux so shatters his own artistic referentials that the resulting textual fragmentation generates a rhythm of appearance and disappearance, and only the lines of passage, a formless All, remain. The counter-life of the Absolute is the dispersed verbal and visual line.

The first two parts of *Moments* continue the experiences felt before Magritte's paintings and recall his earlier response to Paul Klee's work as expressed in the 1954 essay "Aventures de lignes" ("Adventures with Lines," *P*). In *Moments,* the artist is Matta, and Michaux marvels before the constant motion which characterizes Matta's engravings in "The Thin Man" (written in 1957) and "Droites libérées" ("Liberated Lines," dated 1973). Michaux's fascination with Matta's work (as with Magritte's and Klee's) lies in its effect on his inner space. In Matta's engravings, the individual lines are so segmented and so divided that the parts actually change position before the eye in a constant dislocation of the viewer's perspective. The very flux of their appearance composes a mandala of harmony: "Celui qui est né dans la nuit / souvent refera son Mandala" ("He who is born in night / will often redo his Mandala," *MO*, p. 12). Matta's genius projects unity through linear disruptions and invasion of the particular.

The creation of shapelessness through linear dispersal also changes the reader's perspective in the third section, "Ombres pour l'éternité" ("Shadows for Eternity"). Michaux's use of the slash mark to emphasize the alignment of the parts and to obscure their differences suggests, by its appearance on the page, a singleness of effort, a unity of composition. The oblique evocation of shadows guarantees the passage from separation into verbal alliance (since shadows depend upon the contrast between light and dark, yet are neither light nor dark). Repeating throughout the text the term *Semblables* (*similar*), Michaux evokes such parallels that all distinctions and delineations (where does a shadow begin and end?) are dispelled.[1]

The one-dimensional linearity of "Ombres pour l'éternité" continues in "Lignes" ("Lines"), but here it is not a question of the breadth or thickness of lines; details do not matter, just their length, their general character: "Echappées des prisons reçues en héritage, venues non pour définir, mais pour indéfinir . . . de-ci de-là, lignes . . . qui délivrent" ("Escaped from inherited prisons, having come not to define but to undefine . . . here and there, lines . . . which free," *MO*, p. 30). In the fifth part, "Apparitions-Disparitions" ("Appearances-Disappearances"), the dissolution of material reference points, especially of spatial dimensions through the opposition of figures of structuration — lines —, transforms objects from obstacles into agents of unity: "Inondé de vérité / tout soulève / tout est véhicule" ("Inundated with truth / everything lifts up / everything is a vehicle," *MO*, p. 52). By placing objective shapes in motion, Michaux destroys shape and leaves in its passing the sensation of motion. As vibration gains momentum, the particular gives way to the general in an active unveiling of union with formlessness. Hence, the inclusion in *Moments* of the 1959 mescaline text, *Paix dans les brisements,* of "Iniji" from the 1962 volume *Vents et poussières*, and of the 1966 work *Vers la complétude*, as parts six, seven, and eight, demonstrates the desire for union and its ultimate fulfillment through fragmentation: "Entre les lignes de l'Univers un microbe est pris" ("Between the lines of the Universe, a microbe is caught," *MO*, p. 96). Michaux's equation of *flux* and *afflux* rhythmically epitomizes his creative drama, as new meanings constantly emerge from repeated crossings and criss-crossings of his verbal and visual lines of expression. The text "Lieux, moments, traversées du temps" ("Places, Moments, Passages of Time") captures Michaux's joy at having known varied but privileged moments of ascent into a matrix of complete detachment from space and time. Even ultimate silence, represented by Michaux's meditation on Paul Celan's death in "Le Jour, les jours, la fin des jours" ("Birth, Life, Death") offers a special moment in its release of artistic creation.

"Yantra," the text which closes *Moments*, expresses Michaux's conviction that all lines which trace his inner space exploration are like the spokes of a wheel which radiate from his central terrain: "Cercles de l'omniprésente conjonction mâle-femelle/Labyrinthes où s'insinuent et serpentent / les impératives Lampes / de l'alphabet de la langue des dieux" ("Spheres of the omnipresent male-female conjunction / Labyrinths in which penetrate and wind / the imperative Lamps / of the alphabet of the language of the gods," *MO*, p. 129). Because of the many and diverse directions taken by his lines, they are the instrument — yantra — of his inner space which gathers together all vibrations into an accord of self: "Dessin pour retour en absolu. Dessin-destin" ("Design for a return into the absolute. Destiny-Drawing," *MO*, p. 131). Even the very arrangement of the text on the page reflects both dispersal and reunion, for the poem "Yantra" may be read as a conjunction of the differing elements which mark the Michaux creative passage.

Complete from all its angles, comprehensive in all its forms, and dynamic in its reassembly, Michaux's yantra forges the ultimate form beyond all forms: the mandala. Immobile beyond all forces of energy in its composite of all lines, it contains all possibilities of shape, the principle of life. The promise of *Ecuador* to make the earth round ("La terre n'est pas ronde, pas encore, non, il faut la faire ronde," *E*, p. 81) is finally fulfilled, as the circle is squared and the absolute is grasped.

II *Conclusion*

Michaux's passage from disassembly to reassembly is graphically rendered by his own exploration of his creative pathway in *Emergences-Résurgences* (1972). The drawings which he selects as signposts of his experiments in the painting of poetry reflect the *désagrégation-réagrégation* pattern which he himself notes. The opening sketch (*E-R*, p. 8) which dates from 1927 is no more than a zig-zagging of lines which at first glance resembles a rather childish attempt to draw but which neither stimulates the spectator nor orients the painter in any given direction. However, this seemingly aimless drawing so defies all attempts at description, let alone definition, that it effectively captures Michaux's impatience with a verbal culture: "Je peins *pour me déconditionner*" ("I paint *in order to decondition myself*," *E-R*, p. 9). The second sketch (*E-R*, p. 10) is ironically entitled a narration, for it consists of no more than a series of five scribbled lines, executed in the manner of a child who is trying to express himself in script for the first time: "Il me vient une envie de dessiner, de participer au monde par des lignes" ("I feel an urge to sketch, to participate in the world through lines," *E-R*, p. 11). Signs, heads, the *homme-flagellum* of *Mouvements*, gestures, mescaline spectacles, hallucinogenic phenomena, psychedelic drawings, and an even greater range of techniques and materials (black on white, white on black, pastels, watercolors, oils, pen, brush) trace the vastness of Michaux's plastic art, for no method or terrain is left unexplored. Michaux's more recent experiments with acrylic painting and with unusual combinations of media (India ink and acrylic, ink and oil) testify to his on-going graphic transcription of the completeness of existence on one's inner terrain. And, just as his visual renditions of the displacement of outer space and its replacement by inner space form a continuum in his painting, so the same pattern holds true in Michaux's written texts.

In his most recent prose study, *Face à ce qui se dérobe (Facing What is Disappearing,* 1975), Michaux returns to the problem of referential structures which so characterize outer space that they tend to modify inner space. Because this work is based on the same displacement-replacement pattern which identifies *Emergences-Résurgences, Face à ce qui se dérobe* may be said to represent a résumé of Michaux's written passage from rupture to reassembly. Divided into six sections, the first part of *Face à ce qui se dérobe* begins with an outer space situation and a biographical event: "Bras cassé" ("Broken Arm"), which is, in turn, divided into two temporal parts. In 1957, Michaux did break his right arm and was forced to learn to become left-handed. The state of physical suffering with its accompanying psychological discomfort necessitates new gestures in order to respond to a new situation: "Comment dissoudre ma souffrance?" ("How to dissolve my suffering?" *FSD*, p. 41). Michaux notes that he is on such unnatural terrain that even his judgment is affected. Years after the experience, he finds that a right-left balance has been restored; he is no longer either right- or left-handed, but physically ambidextrous and psychologically symmetrical. The emergence of his left-hand experience has brought about a corporeal counterbalance: "L'ensemble droite-gauche, une des nombreuses divisions de l'être, division à garder qui est aussi réunion" ("The right-left set, one of the numerous divisions of the human being, a division to be maintained which is also reunion," *FSD*, p. 66). Reaffirming intervention as an effective counter-action to the hostile situation, Michaux displaces actual suffering and replaces it by a new and triumphant sense of balance.

As the possessions of *Mes Propriétés* resurge intact in the physical experience of "Bras cassé," so the imaginary journeys of *Ailleurs* and the transformative hallucinations of the drug texts recur in the second section, "Relations avec les apparitions" ("Relations With Visions"): "En tout homme . . . il doit y avoir flux incessant et incapacité de demeurer immobile, parfaitement stable" ("In every man . . . there must be incessant flux and the incapacity to stay immobile, perfectly stable," *FSD*, p. 74). It is never a question of using the imagination to animate inanimate objects as a means of transforming the outer world, for to do so would be to affirm the multiple shape of the external situation. On the contrary, Michaux seeks to generate substance itself and create energy where there is no energy: "A défaire un certain état statique" ("To destroy a certain static state," *FSD*, p. 85). Yet even his gestures tend to localize his situation. Consequently, relations with the appearances of things demand their disappearance, a constantly changing spectacle; otherwise, there is only the exchange of one situation for another: "Le geste malgré moi inducteur suscite, continue à susciter des formes — dont je ne veux pas, et qui m'encombrent, me déséquilibrent, me ramènent de la matière feutrée, voilée" ("The gestures, inductive against my will, create, continue to create forms — which I don't want and which crowd me, disorient me, pull me out of the noiseless, veiled matter," *FSD*, p. 87). Any attempt to establish a relationship with an object maintains and perpetuates outer space.

Turning from the experience of sight and touch to that of sound in "Dans l'eau changeante des résonances" ("In the Changing Water of Resonances"), Michaux finds in primitive African sanzas, for example, the reversal of musical composition, that is, no precision, just the passage of fragmentary sounds. The vibration of rhythm, as captured graphically by Michaux in his 1974 *Par la voie des rythmes*, is a freeing of the individual in one sense, but it still belongs to another's terrain, not one's own. Nonetheless, the experience of listening to music[2] is the experience of a movement which is the opposite of Michaux's own and leads in the fourth section, "Survenue de la contemplation" ("Unexpected Arrival of Contemplation"), to a state of repose which is beyond intervention: "Etre très *éveillé* et suprêmement *détaché*. Il faut cesser, j'avais cessé d'être investigateur" ("To be quite *awake* and supremely *detached*. It is necessary to cease, I had ceased being an investigator," *FSD*, p. 113). The very silence which follows listening to music is a displacement of space, of demobilized thought ("Penser démobilisé," *FSD*, p. 113), which renounces reflection: "Pas de référence dans la contemplation. Voir, mais pas examiner" ("No reference in contemplation. To see, but not examine," *FSD*, p. 113). This silence is a counter-life of non-situation, a permanence beyond words and gestures which reassembles all the passages of his life into a solidarity of identity: "Non pas en passant, mais comme si à la manière d'une partie d'assemblage, j'avais été enclenché dedans. / Accru, nouveau, total" ("Not in passing, but as if in the fashion of an assembly-line, I had been locked in. / Enhanced, new, total," *FSD*, p. 117). This complete concentration on non-participation in order to preserve every form and every element is the experience of temporal and spatial detachment: "Dégagement de l'espace local et de la durée momentanée. / Arrivé là où il n'y a plus d'impulsion propre" ("Disengagement from local space and from momentary duration. / Arrival where there is no longer any inherent impulse," *FSD*, p. 122). Contemplation is the all-inclusive assembly of the parts, but assembled freely, spontaneously, without respect for motivation, stimulation,[3] desire, interest, or appetite. It is the psychological yantra of the immutable grandeur of inner space. The power of contemplation is its generation of the experience of being a mandala: perfect, pure, complete, harmonious, permanent.

The last two parts of *Face à ce qui se dérobe* represent two examples of the power of contemplation. In "Arrivée à Alicante" ("Arrival at Alicante"), extreme physical fatigue makes movement so difficult that the multiple aspects of the world seem solid and in place. A calm reigns because the personality is too tired to delineate, reflect, sort out relationships; demobilization of thought processes and reactions displaces the admixture of an outer space situation and replaces it with conjunction. In "Moriturus," Michaux presents an allegory about a traveler, N....[4] N.... keeps traveling a given tortuous road; on his journey, each time he reacts outwardly to an obstacle, the surrounding landscape becomes more difficult to cross. When the mountain makes a sign to him, it takes on form and threatens his outer existence. But N... continues, only to slip on a rock and be mortally wounded, unable to move. In his dying moments, a strain of music is heard, then a silence, then a voice promising rebirth. N... has reached perfection at the end of his journey, but, in the midst of this moment, he makes a gesture, a small movement which dispels the magic of the moment and returns him to his hostile situation. He dies, as the referentials of outer space vanquish the joy of inner existence.

Contemplation, then, emerges as the final ring in Michaux's spiral: "Le pouvoir de contemplation peut être vérifié de loin en loin par la confrontation avec une image ou un mot" ("The power of contemplation can be verified from time to time through confrontation with an image or a word," *FSD*, p. 124). As his spiral of emergence-resurgence continues to contract in a concentrated impulse of generative energy and releases a mandala of the formless All, Michaux opens the locks to the space within and invites his reader-spectator to follow his path of rhythmic flux and fragmentation, which extend man's vision beyond the limits of space and time. By facing what is disappearing (limits, forms, recognizable shapes), Michaux also suggests what is appearing, for exorcism of the parts does not destroy; it displaces and rearranges them. The final return to base is the regaining of self-sovereignty, the ultimate Michaux destination in his artistic adventure. While perhaps only the design of the mandala adequately expresses the experience of the absolute, nevertheless, Michaux's work captures through a continuous pattern of disintegration and reintegration the substance of life in all its forms. The design of destiny is the contemplation of human expression of self in all its possibilities: prose, painting, poetry.

Notes and References

References for the quotations used in this study follow the quotation in parentheses, and the works under discussion have been abbreviated as follows: *A (Ailleurs); AT (Arbre des Tropiques); BA (Un Barbare en Asie); CG (Connaissance par les gouffres); E (Ecuador); EDD (L'Espace du dedans); EE (Epreuves, exorcismes); E-R (Emergences-Résurgences); FE (Façons d'endormi, façons d'éveillé); FSD (Face à ce qui se dérobe); FV (Face aux verrous); GE (Les Grandes Epreuves de l'esprit et les innombrables petites); IT (L'Infini turbulent); M (Mouvements); MM (Misérable Miracle); MO (Moments: Traversées du temps); NR (La Nuit remue); P (Passages); PA (Poteaux d'angle); PB (Paix dans les brisements); PE (Peintures); PLI (Plume précédé de Lointain intérieur); QCH (Quatre Cents Hommes en croix); QJF (Qui je fus); VC (Vers la complétude); VEP (Vents et poussières); VP (La Vie dans les plis).*

Unless otherwise indicated, all editions used are the most recent ones as listed in the bibliography.

Chapter One

1. All translations follow as closely as possible the original French and are my own. Obvious cognates have not been translated.

2. A complete biography of Henri Michaux has yet to be published. However, what is known about Michaux the man has been faithfully summarized in this chapter, in keeping with Michaux's own approach to the unity between his life and work.

Chapter Two

1. The date 1925 is that given by Michaux in *Emergences-Résurgences*: "La peinture tout à coup à vingt-six ans me parut propre à saper mon état et mon univers" ("Suddenly at age 26 painting seemed right to me for undermining my state and my universe," p. 116).

2. In *Face à ce qui ce dérobe* (1975), Michaux presents fatigue in a beneficial light. Other contradictions also occur, but his attitude towards fatigue is perhaps the most interesting in terms of the number of pages devoted by Michaux to this subject.

3. "Glu et gli" is usually read as a nonsense text which demonstrates Michaux's war on language. The full version of the poem has not been reprinted since the original publication, which included an additional two stanzas — or another half of the poem. This last half of the original text is linguistically and thematically composed in traditional terms and confirms the reading I have given it here. Indeed, in an attempt to follow, however roughly, a chronological line, this is the only reading possible: that is, a reading of the complete text.

4. While *Mes Propriétés* was originally published as a separate volume in 1930, it became the second section of *La Nuit remue* in 1935; and this definitive edition is the one used for the discussion in this chapter.

5. Michaux occasionally uses a foreign language in his titles; the subtitle to his first work, *Les Rêves et la jambe*, is in English ("A Philosophical and Literary Essay"), just as the title for *Ecuador* is in Spanish. While the use of foreign terms reflects, of course, his linguistic ability and travels, it also reveals his deep interest in language as expression. In *Mes Propriétés*, language emerges as a possession.

6. These are imaginary names for imaginary animals and, as such, I have not translated them.

7. "Rubililieuse" is a nonsense term coined by Michaux; its sonority attests to an undefinable, but no less existent and felt inner force.

Chapter Three

1. These five texts are "Un Homme paisible" ("A Peaceful Man"), which was first titled "La Philosophie de Plume" ("Plume's Philosophy") in 1930; "Plume voyage" ("Plume Travels"); "Plume au restaurant" ("Plume at the Restaurant"); "Dans les appartements de la reine" ("In the Queen's Apartments"); and "La Vision de Plume" ("Plume's Vision"). Unless otherwise noted, I refer to the 1966 edition of *Plume précédé de Lointain intérieur*.

2. All seven texts appear in *L'Espace du dedans* as *Plume* texts.

3. Pon is one of Michaux's earliest fictive characters. The name is based on the verb *pondre, to lay eggs*.

4. *Un Certain Plume* is a specific collection of thirteen prose texts, but only one part of *Plume*. The name Plume is based on feather (or pen) and reinforces the weightlessness which marks these texts, while the name Pon in *Difficultés* suggests shape and weight (egg).

5. Quoted by Robert Bréchon in his *Michaux* (Paris: Gallimard, 1959), p. 205.

6. The other two texts of the 1930 *Trois Nuits* become part of *Difficultés* and are listed as *Plume* texts in *L'Espace du dedans*.

7. "Ces apparitions ne sont pas des anges. Ce n'est pas Dieu, non plus, il semble. Peut-être c'est la gestation de la nuit essentielle, la nuit qui luit

nuit et jour, la nuit de ceux à qui le jour ne donne rien" ("These appearances are not angels. It is not God, either, it seems. Perhaps it is the gestation of eternal night, night which shines night and day, the night of those to whom day gives nothing").

8. The term *bren* is a synonym for excrement.

9. It is possible to read this play as a commentary on God, Who would then be aligned with the lunatics on the side of fantasy, in opposition to the harsh reality of suffering. On the other hand, the rejection of the real leads to an affirmative view of God, acceptable because belief in a deity brings relief. In either case, engagement and confrontation are repudiated.

10. In the expanded volume of *La Nuit remue, Mes Propriétés* follows the texts of *La Nuit remue*.

11. Michaux has written two different texts by this title, but this one is the less well-known. The second one, also in prose, appears at the end of the *Poèmes* section of *La Nuit remue* and ends the volume. It is the second text which is included in *L'Espace du dedans*. However, both texts are dated 1934.

12. It should be noted that references to drugs appear in Michaux's work as early as *Les Rêves et la jambe* (1923), while his first mention of drug usage is found in *Ecuador* (1929) and one of the stimulants mentioned is ether.

Chapter Four

1. The 1936 volume opens with five untitled but numbered texts which appear as a separate introductory section; the title page on *Entre centre et absence* is placed next and is followed by the rest of the texts. When *Entre centre et absence* becomes part of *Lointain intérieur* in 1938, the opening five texts are collectively entitled "Magie" ("Magic"), and the text "Entre centre et absence," originally the opening one, becomes the closing text.

2. *La Ralentie* was also published separately in 1937.

3. "Paix égale" ("Even Peace"), "Pensées" ("Thoughts"), "Le Grand Violon" ("The Great Violin"), and "Vieillesse" ("Old Age").

4. One cannot help but see in these texts a refutation of the "new humanism" and "new heroism" which characterize French literature in the 1930's. Michaux remains suspicious of collective thought and individual heroism which are first based on confrontation and engagement with outer space and, second, are absolutes despite all efforts to make them concrete.

5. Michaux's 1948 preface to *Un Barbare en Asie*.

6. While Michaux remains fascinated by oriental culture, his attraction is not the result of this trip as he evokes it in 1933. Although the Asian experience continues to emerge, the work *Un Barbare en Asie* is untouched by any conversion (artistic, philosophical, religious); it is a highly detached work of objective observation.

7. Curiously, this listing does indeed describe Michaux's own work after the experience. The rings of each spiral after 1933 are heightened by his Asian adventures in an on-going emergence-resurgence pattern.

8. Michaux's preface to the 1948 edition of *Ailleurs*.

Chapter Five

1. The sole exception is possibly the novel, yet *Un Certain Plume* could be interpreted as an anti-novel or as a parody of the novel form. Certainly, all narrative techniques associated with both the traditional and new novel forms can be found in Michaux's work.

2. "Qui il est" ("Who He Is"), *PE*, n.p. This 1939 introduction is later considerably revised as the essay "Peindre" ("To Paint," *Passages*, pp. 83-85). The lines quoted here do not appear in the revised version. Although Michaux uses the impersonal third person singular form in "Qui il est" (which in "Peindre" he changes to the first person singular), there remains the allusion to his earlier volume *Qui je fus*. In 1939, then, it would appear that Michaux finds who he is (as opposed to the who he was), but, by 1950, the date of the first publication of the revised essay in *Passages*, he has detected his own pattern of emergence-resurgence, hence the new title, "Peindre."

3. "Qui il est"; the last line of this quotation ("Une vie toute inventée") is deleted in 1950.

4. For Michaux's rejection of portraiture, see his "En pensant au phénomène de la peinture" ("On Thinking About the Phenomenon of Painting"), *Passages*, especially pp. 88-104, which represent the complete 1946 introduction to *Peintures et dessins*.

5. Textually, there are definite references to this event, and in *Emergences-Résurgences* Michaux explicitly cites their historical basis (pp. 22-31). Other external situations, such as his travels and the loss of his wife, also serve as bases for artistic reaction in his work.

6. The 1939 edition is unpaginated; when citing the texts republished in *L'Espace du dedans* (1966), I have used that work for paginal references.

7. Michaux's selection of *motricité* reaffirms art as the generation of energy. *Motivity* is a biological term which means the power to produce energy. Of additional interest is the fact that the phrase *mots-motricité* does not appear in the original essay, "Qui il est," but was added in the revised "Peindre."

8. There are very few changes; only a total of six texts were omitted from the three original volumes, while four were added in 1945: "Dans mon camp" ("In My Camp"), "Monde" ("World"), "Le Calme," and "Annales." "La Marche dans le tunnel" ("The Walk in the Tunnel") was originally entitled "Le Chant dans le labyrinthe" ("The Song in the Labyrinth") and consisted of only eleven parts instead of twenty-three.

9. Preface to the 1943 edition of *Exorcismes*; these lines were deleted in 1945.

10. *Epreuves, exorcismes* consists of forty-two texts; the first twenty-five are a mixture from *Exorcismes* (1943) and *Labyrinthes* (1944); the last seventeen texts are from *Le Lobe des monstres* (1944).

Chapter Six

1. *Passages* is the title of Michaux's 1950 and 1963 collection of essays which contain his studies of his artistic journey. Election of passage (motion) over being and the choice of title for a volume of essays which is unified first by this theme and second by a linking together of painting as the structural element recall Montaigne's *Essais*: "Je ne peints pas l'estre. Je peints le passage" ("I do not portray being. I portray passing," *Du repentir — On Repentence*, III:2).

2. Unfolding (*déplier*) is another major textual resurgence in Michaux's work; earlier, in *Au pays de La Magie*, he declares: "Il s'agit de la [situation] déplier" ("It is a matter of unfolding the situation," *A*, p. 258).

3. "Signes," *XXe Siècle* (January 1954), 47.

4. *Ibid.*, 49.

5. *Moments: Traversées du temps* includes all of Michaux's poetry written between 1951 and 1973.

6. Because only the 1951 edition of *Mouvements* contains the drawings and the postface, it is the volume used in my discussion. Because this work is not paginated, I have used the *Face aux verrous* volume when quoting from the poem "Mouvements."

7. In "Signes," Michaux regrets that his figures in *Mouvements* express gestures and not signs. In the strict sense, then, gestures are movements, but related to a situation, while signs are free from situations. In *Emergences-Résurgences*, he maintains this distinction, as he reveals that his own passage from disobedience to modification is unified by the search for a pure sign.

8. The drawings for *Quatre Cents Hommes en croix* are dated 1953, between *Mouvements* and "Signes."

Chapter Seven

1. The 1972 edition includes an Addenda and so is used here.

2. "Vitesse et tempo" is republished as "Dessiner l'écoulement du temps" ("Sketching the Flow of Time") in *Passages*.

3. For an excellent study of Michaux's scientific approach to drugs, see Olivier Loras, *Rencontre avec Henri Michaux au plus profond des gouffres* (Paris: J. et S. Bleyon, 1967).

4. Michaux's experiments with drugs never include drugs which he considers addictive: ". . .la tentation pourrait venir de juger dorénavant l'ensemble de mes écrits, comme l'oeuvre d'un drogué. Je regrette. Je suis plutôt du type buveur d'eau. Jamais d'alcool. Pas d'excitants, et depuis des années pas de café, pas de tabac, pas de thé. De loin en loin du vin, et peu. Depuis toujours, et de tout ce qui se prend, peu. Prendre et s'abstenir. Surtout s'abstenir. La fatigue est ma drogue, si l'on veut savoir" (". . .one might be tempted hereafter to judge the whole of my writings, as the work of a drug addict. I am sorry. I am rather the type who drinks water. Never alcohol. No stimulants, and for years no coffee, no tobacco, no tea. From time to time wine, and little. Forever, and with regard to everything one can take, little. To take and to abstain. Especially abstention. Fatigue is my drug, if you want to know," *MM*, p. 170).

5. These two essays are available only in the original 1959 edition of *Paix dans les brisements*.

6. "Iniji" is republished in *Moments: Traversées du temps* (1973).

Chapter Eight

1. Literally and figuratively, the slash mark becomes a shadow on the printed page.

2. Music is another of Michaux's interests. Many texts refer to music in one form or another (the experience of listening to music, as well as the use of musical terms), most notably his poem "Le Grand Violon" (*Lointain intérieur*) and his essay "Un Certain Phénomène qu'on appelle musique" ("A Certain Phenomenon Called Music," *Passages*). Music may, indeed, surge in a future Michaux spiral; certainly, the coiling process has begun.

3. Inherent in Michaux's dissatisfaction with drugs is their failure to permit contemplation: "Aussi est-elle [la mescaline] l'ennemi de la poésie, de la méditation, et surtout du mystère" ("Consequently, mescaline is the enemy of poetry, of meditation, and especially of mystery," *MM*, p. 64).

4. N... is an unnamed and undescribed persona who occasionally appears in Michaux's work. An abstracted character, N... can be viewed as a who-I-might-have-been-if figure, as opposed to Plume, Pon, and others who are purely fictive characters for counter-action.

Selected Bibliography

PRIMARY SOURCES

The place of publication is Paris unless otherwise stated. I have subdivided collected works and noted the place and date of publication for the pre-published sections.

1923 *Les Rêves et la jambe,* Antwerp: Ça ira.
      Fables des origines, Brussels: Le Disque Vert.
1927 *Qui je fus,* N.R.F.
1929 *Ecuador,* Gallimard; revised edition, 1968.
1930 *Trois Nuits,* Gallimard.
1933 *Un Barbare en Asie,* Gallimard; revised editions, 1945, 1967.
1935 *La Nuit remue,* Gallimard; revised edition, 1967.
      La Nuit remue.
      Mes Propriétés, J.O. Fourcade, 1929.
1938 *Plume précédé de Lointain intérieur,* Gallimard; revised editions, 1963, 1967.
      Lointain intérieur.
      Entre centre et absence, H. Matarasso, 1936.
      La Ralentie, G.L.M., 1937.
      Animaux fantastiques.
      L'Insoumis.
      Je vous écris d'un pays lointain.
      Poèmes.
      Difficultés.
      Plume.
      Un Certain Plume, Editions du Carrefour, 1930.
      Chaînes.
1939 *Peintures,* G.L.M.
1942 *Arbre des Tropiques,* Gallimard.
1945 *Epreuves, exorcismes,* Gallimard; revised edition, 1967.
      Exorcismes, Robert J. Godet, 1943.
      Labyrinthes, Robert J. Godet, 1944.
      Le Lobe des monstres, Lyons: L'Arbalète, 1944.
      L'Espace du dedans, Gallimard; revised edition, 1966.
1946 *Peintures et dessins,* Le Point du jour.

1948   *Nous deux encore,* J. Lambert.
       Ailleurs, Gallimard; revised editions, 1961, 1967.
       Voyage en Grande Garabagne, Gallimard, 1936.
       Au pays de La Magie, Gallimard, 1941.
       Ici, Poddema, Lausanne: H.L. Mermod, 1946.
1949   *La Vie dans les plis,* Gallimard, 1949.
       Liberté d'action, Fontaine, 1945.
       Apparitions, Le Point du jour, 1946.
       Meidosems, Le Point du jour, 1948.
       Lieux inexprimables.
       Vieillesse de Pollagoras.
1950   *Passages,* Le Point du jour; revised edition, 1963.
       Arriver à se réveiller, St.-Martin d'Etelan: Pierre Bettencourt.
1954   *Face aux verrous,* Gallimard; revised edition, 1967.
       Mouvements, Gallimard, 1951.
       Poésie pour pouvoir, René Drouin, 1949.
       Tranches de savoir suivi du Secret de la situation politique,
           Librairie Les Pas Perdus, 1950.
       Nouvelles de l'étranger, Mercure de France, 1952.
1956   *Quatre Cents Hommes en croix,* St.-Martin d'Etelan: Pierre Bet-
       tencourt.
       Misérable Miracle, Monaco: Editions du Rocher; revised edition,
       Gallimard, 1972.
1957   *L'Infini turbulent,* Mercure de France; revised edition, 1964.
1959   *Paix dans les brisements,* Flinker.
1961   *Connaissance par les gouffres,* Gallimard; revised edition, 1967.
1962   *Vents et poussières,* Flinker.
1966   *Les Grandes Epreuves de l'esprit et les innombrables petites,* Le
       Point du jour.
1967   *Vers la complétude,* G.L.M.
1969   *Façons d'endormi, façons d'éveillé,* Le Point du jour.
1971   *Poteaux d'angle,* L'Herne.
1972   *Emergences-Résurgences,* Geneva: Albert Skira.
       En rêvant à partir de peintures énigmatiques, Fata Morgana.
1973   *Moments: Traversées du temps,* Gallimard.
1974   *Par la voie des rythmes,* Fata Morgana.
1975   *Face à ce qui se dérobe,* Gallimard.
1976   *Henri Michaux: Peintures,* Fondation Maeght.

SECONDARY SOURCES

A.   *Books*

BEGUELIN, MARIANNE. *Henri Michaux: Esclave et démiurge.* Lausanne:
       L'Age d'homme, 1974. Belabored effort to treat Michaux's work un-

der the aegis of the ecstasy of suffering, the law of domination-subordination.

BELLOUR, RAYMOND, ed. *Henri Michaux.* Paris: L'Herne, 1966. Uneven and generally unexciting group of essays, most of them published elsewhere; bibliography marked by substantial errors.

――――. *Henri Michaux, ou une mesure de l'être.* Paris: Gallimard, 1965. Rich source for information on Michaux and interesting philosophical approach to Michaux's work.

BERTELÉ, RENÉ. *Henri Michaux.* Paris: Seghers, Poèmes d'aujourd'hui, 1957. First published in 1946, still serves as important general overview of Michaux's poetry and provides good introduction to his work.

BOWIE, MALCOLM. *Henri Michaux: A Study of His Literary Works.* Oxford: Clarendon Press, 1973. Sound examination of major texts; bibliography is outstanding.

BRÉCHON, ROBERT. *Michaux.* Paris: Gallimard, 1959. Pertinent to any study on Michaux although limited by a point of view that finds pessimism at every turn.

DADOUN, ROGER, ed. *Ruptures sur Henri Michaux.* Paris: Payot, 1976. Interesting collection of five essays, which emphasize a poetics that energizes the insignificant.

GIDE, ANDRÉ. *Découvrons Henri Michaux.* Paris: Gallimard, 1941. First full-length study; usefulness limited.

LORAS, OLIVIER. *Rencontre avec Henri Michaux au plus profond des gouffres.* Paris: J. et S. Bleyon, 1967. Incisive study of Michaux's drug experimentations; best work to date on this subject.

MURAT, N. *Henri Michaux.* Paris: Editions Universitaires, 1967. Short, penetrating study; highly teleological in orientation.

PLACE, GEORGES. *Henri Michaux.* Paris: Chroniques des Lettres Françaises, 1969. Useful biographical data and bibliography despite errors.

B. *Articles of Particular Interest*

BELAVAL, YVON. "Henri Michaux. Une Magie rationnelle," *Les Temps Modernes* (September 1951), 449-59.

――――. "Introduction à la poésie expérimentale," *Critique,* 18 (1962), 913-28.

BELLOUR, RAYMOND. "La Double Enigme," *Les Temps Modernes* (April 1965), 1903-12.

BISHOP, LLOYD. "Michaux's 'Clown,' " *French Review,* 36 (1962), 152-57.

BLANCHOT, MAURICE. "L'Infini et l'infini," *La Nouvelle Nouvelle Revue Française* (January 1958), 98-110.

BONNEFOI, GENEVIÈVE. "Henri Michaux ou le démon de la connaissance," *Les Lettres Nouvelles* (November 1961), 116-23.

————. "Michaux l'insaisissable," in *Henri Michaux, Peintures* (Paris: Adrian Maeght, 1976), pp. 15-27.

————. " 'Le Petit Cortège' d'Henri Michaux," *Les Lettres Nouvelles* (July-August 1956), 131-37.

BOUNOURE, GABRIEL. "Le Darçana d'Henri Michaux," *La Nouvelle Nouvelle Revue Française* (May, June 1957), 875-83, 1074-84.

BRÉCHON, ROBERT. "Parcours d'Henri Michaux," *Critique,* 13 (1957), 819-28.

BROOME, PETER. "Henri Michaux and Failure in Mescalin," *Australian Journal of French Studies,* 2 (1964), 188-220.

————. "The Introversion of Henri Michaux: His Aims, Techniques and Shortcomings," *Nottingham French Studies,* 1 (1962), 34-44.

————. "Michaux and the Exorcism on God," *Australian Journal of French Studies,* 2 (1965), 191-220.

DARRAULT, IVAN. "*La Ralentie.* Essai de description sémantique," *Promesse* (Winter 1967), 8-36.

DEGUY, MICHEL. "L'Autopsie," *Promesse* (Winter 1967), 46-48.

DUPIN, JACQUES. "Contemplatif en action," in *Henri Michaux: Peintures* (Paris: Adrian Maeght, 1976), pp. 3-12.

GUENIER, N. "La Création lexicale chez Henri Michaux," *Cahiers Lexicologie,* 11 (1967), 75-87.

HACKETT, C.A. "Michaux and Plume," *French Studies,* 17 (1963), 40-49.

HOOG, ARMAND. "Henri Michaux or Mythic Symbolism," *Yale French Studies* (Spring 1952), 143-54.

KUHN, REINHARD. "The Hermeneutics of Silence: Michaux and Mescaline," *Yale French Studies,* 50 (1974), 130-41.

KUSHNER, EVA. "L'Humour de Michaux," *French Review,* 40 (1967), 495-504.

LA CHARITÉ, VIRGINIA A. "Dis-Order and Unity in the Work of Henri Michaux," *Modern Language Review,* 72 (1977), forthcoming.

LE CLÉZIO, J.M.G. "Sur Henri Michaux," *Cahiers du Sud* (November-December 1964), 262-69.

MAGNY, OLIVIER DE. "Ecriture de l'impossible," *Les Lettres Nouvelles* (February 1963), 123-38.

MILLS, RALPH J. "Char and Michaux: Magicians of Insecurity," *Chicago Review,* 15 (1961), 40-56.

ONIMUS, JEAN. "Henri Michaux. Peur et poésie," in *Expériences de la poésie* (Paris: Desclée de Brouwer, 1973), pp. 44-59.

PEYNARD, JEAN. "Une Approche d'Henri Michaux," *Critique,* 15 (1959), 943-51.

PLEYNET, MARCELIN. "René Char et Henri Michaux dans l'avenir de la parole," *L'Arc* (Spring 1961), 63-67.

TERRASSE, JEAN. "Henri Michaux: de l'être du langage au langage de l'être," *Synthèses* (May 1969), 70-87.

Index

"Adieu à une ville et à une femme," 25
"Adieux d'Anhimaharua," 103
Ailleurs, 18, 20, 31, 54, 64, 70-75, 130
"Alphabet," 87-88, 90
"Amours," 38
"L'Animal mange-serrure," 59
Animaux fantastiques, 55, 62-63
"L'Année maudite," 86
aphorisms, 19, 20, 26, 101, 126
"Apparition," 96
Apparitions, 18, 95-97
"Apparitions-Disparitions," 127-28
"Après l'accident," 103
Arbre des Tropiques, 91-92
"L'Arrachage des têtes," 44
"Arrivée à Alicante," 132
Arriver à se reveiller, 18-19
"Articulations," 38
Asian trip, 17, 70-71, 73
Au Pays de La Magie, 18, 70, 72, 74
"L'Auto de l'Avenue de l'Opéra," 50
"Avenir," 69-70
"Aventures de lignes," 127

Barbare en Asie, Un, 17, 20, 70, 71-72, 73, 75, 137
Breton, André, 23
"Bonheur bête," 50
"Le Bourreau," 60

"Cahiers d'Orga, signés d'Orga," 116
"Caillou courant," 27
"Calme," 89
Celan, Paul, 128
Certain Plume, Un, 17, 40, 42-46, 47, 65, 70, 72, 74, 136, 138
Chaînes enchaînées," 37
"Champ de ma conscience, Le," 116
"Chant de mort," 40
Chaplin, Charlie, 22-23

Cheronnet, Louis, 79
"Chronique d'aiguilleur," 22
"Clown," 81-82, 83
"Combats," 82-83
"Comme je vous vois," 57
"Comme pierre dans la puits," 69
"Compagnons," 38
Connaissance par les gouffres, 19, 113-15, 120
"Conseil au sujet de la mer," 49
"Conseil au sujet des pins," 49
"Conseils," 38
"Contre!" 51, 53
"Couché," 83
"Craquements, Les," 86

"Dans la compagnie des monstres," 87
"Dans la Nuit," 67
"Dans le cercle brisant de la jeune magicienne," 103
"Dans les appartements de la reine," 43
"Déchéance," 50
"Demain n'est pas encore," 103
"Dessins commentés," 49-50
Difficultés, 40-42, 43, 46, 47, 70, 136
"Dimanche à la campagne," 60
"Dragon," 82
Drame des constructeurs, Le, 17, 40, 46-47, 70
dreams, 20, 49, 123-24
"Droites libérées," 127
drugs, 19, 20, 50-51, 107-20, 121, 122-23, 130-31, 137, 140

"Ecce homo," 87
Ecuador, 17, 28, 29, 30, 31
Ecuador, 17, 28-32, 33, 35, 36-37, 51, 62, 75, 107, 129, 136, 137
Emergences-Résurgences, 20, 105, 121, 122, 129, 139

145

"Emportez-moi," 38
energy, 49, 76-92, 93, 98, 100, 103, 116, 131
"Enigmes," 25
"En respirant," 49
En rêvant à partir de peintures énigmatiques, 125-26
Entre centre et absence, 17, 55, 56-62, 65, 78, 137
"Entre centre et absence," 57-58
"L'Epoque des Illuminés," 26, 27
Epreuves, exorcismes, 18, 77, 85-91, 113, 139
Espace aux ombres, L', 102
Espace du dedans, L', 18, 20, 40, 65, 126, 136, 137
"Etapes," 49
"Ether, L'," 50-51
"étranger parle, L'," 101
"Eux," 38
"Examinateur — Midi —," 27
exorcism, 85-88, 93, 104
Exorcismes, 18, 85, 139

Fables des origines, 22, 23
Face à ce qui se dérobe, 20, 122, 130-32, 135
Face aux verrous, 19, 20, 93, 94, 98-103, 106
Façons d'endormi, façons d'éveillé, 20, 122, 123-25
Faits divers, 102
"femme me demande conseil, Une," 59
"Fils de morne," 27-28, 34
Fin d'un domaine, 99, 102-103
"Fin d'un domaine," 103
"Fort, Le," 50

Gangotena, Alfredo, 17, 28
"Glu et gli," 27
gong, 32, 37-38
"Grand Combat, Le," 27
"Grand Violon, Le," 67
Grandes Epreuves de l'esprit et les innombrables petites, Les, 19, 117-19, 120

"Homme-bombe," 96

"Homme paisible, Un," 43
"homme qui mange son fils, Un," 22
"Hôte d'honneur de Bren Club, L'," 45
humor, 22, 86

"Icebergs," 52
Ici, Poddema, 18, 70, 72, 74-75
"Immense Voix," 87, 88
"Impossible Retour, L'," 103
Infini turbulent, L', 19, 108, 110-11, 115, 120
"Iniji," 116, 128
Insoumis, L', 55, 63-64
intervention, 35, 39, 42, 45, 46, 50, 51, 53, 58-59, 86, 103
"Intervention," 35
inversion, 43, 51, 112

"Je suis gong," 37
Je vous écris d'un pays lointain, 55, 64-65
"Jour, les jours, la fin des jours, Le," 128

Klee, Paul, 127

"Labyrinthe," 89-90
Labyrinthes, 18, 85, 89, 90, 139
"Lac, Le," 50
"Lazare, tu dors?" 86
"Lettre, La," 88
"Leurs Secrets en spectacle," 115
Liberté d'action, 18, 94-95, 96, 103, 106
"Liberté d'action," 98
Lieux inexprimables, 97-98
"Lieux, moments, traversées du temps," 121
Lobe des monstres, Les, 18, 85, 89, 139
Lointain intérieur, 40, 54, 55-70, 71, 72, 137

"Magie," 58-59
Magritte, René, 125-26, 127
"Mais Toi, quand viendras-tu?" 67-68
mandala, 121-22, 129
"Marche dans le tunnel, La," 86
"Masques du vide, Les," 87
Master of Ho, 88, 89-90, 91

Matta, 127
"Ma Vie," 51
Meidosems, 18, 97
"Mer, La," 87, 90
"Mère de neuf enfants, Une," 44
mescaline, 108-13, 114, 128
"Mes Occupations," 34
Mes Propriétés, 17, 32-38, 40, 48, 72, 130, 136, 137
"Mes Propriétés," 34-35
Misérable Miracle, 19, 107, 108-10, 111, 113, 115, 120
Moments: Traversées du temps, 20, 122, 126-29, 139
"Monde, Le," 88-89
"Mon Roi," 48-49, 50, 53
"Mon Sang," 66
"Moriturus," 132
motion, 93, 100-103, 105, 107, 116, 121
Mouvements, 19, 20, 99-100, 103, 105, 106, 129, 139
"Mouvements de l'être intérieur," 41

"Naissance," 41
"Nature, fidèle à l'homme, La," 60, 61
night, 39, 47-48, 53, 67
"Notes de zoologie," 36
"Nous autres," 51
Nous deux encore, 18, 105
Nouvelles de l'étranger, 19, 99, 101-102
"Nuit des Bulgares, La," 43
"Nuit des disparitions, La," 41
"Nuit des embarras, La," 41
"Nuit des noces, La," 49
Nuit remue, La, 17, 20, 40, 47-53, 137
"Nuit remue, La," 48

"Ombres pour l'éternité," 127
"On cherche querelle à Plume," 43, 45
"On veut voler mon nom," 59

Paix dans les brisements, 19, 20, 108, 111-13, 115, 120, 128
"Paix égale," 66
"Paix des sabres, La," 87, 88
Par la voie des rythmes, 20, 99-100, 105, 131

"Partages de l'homme," 25
Passages, 18, 126
"Paysages," 82
Peintures, 18, 77, 79, 83-84
Peintures et dessins, 18, 77, 80, 83-84, 85, 87, 90, 91
"Pensées," 66
Personnel, 101-102
"Petits Soucis de chacun, Les," 50
plastic art, 16-17, 18, 20, 23-24, 49, 60-62, 76, 77-84, 87-88, 90-92, 96-97, 99-100, 104-106, 109, 111-12, 115-16, 120, 121-22, 125-26, 127, 129-30
Plume, 17, 42-46, 48, 65, 91-92, 136
"Plume à Casablanca," 45
"Plume au plafond," 45
"Plume au restaurant," 43
"Plume avait mal au doigt," 44
"Plume et les culs-de-jatte," 45
Plume précédé de Lointain intérieur, 20, 70
"Plume voyage," 43
Poèmes, 26, 33, 37, 38, 47, 51-53, 55, 65-70
Poésie pour pouvoir, 99, 100-101
Pon, 41, 43, 136
"Portrait d'A," 40, 41
Poteaux d'angle, 20, 122, 126
"Predication," 26
"Prince de la nuit," 82, 83
"Principes d'enfant," 26
prose v. poetry, 47-48, 96-97; poem, 47-48, 65, 96-97

"Quand les motocyclettes rentrent à l'horizon," 60
Quatre Cents Hommes en croix, 93, 94, 103-106
Quelques Jours de ma vie chez les insectes, 101
Qui je fus, 17, 20, 24-28, 29, 32, 138
"Qui je fus," 24-25

"Ra," 38
"Race Urdes, La," 36
. . . *Rait*, 102
Ralentie, La, 55, 62
"Repos dans le malheur," 65-66

"Rêve de Moore," 59
reverie, 20, 21-22, 123-25
Rêves et la jambe, Les, 21-22, 13, 33, 107, 136, 137
"Rodrigue," 38
"Rubilileuse," 38

"Séance de sac, La," 95
Sciences naturelles, 33, 36-37
"Signes," 99
spectacle, 34-35
"Sphinx, Les," 89
"Sportif au lit, Le," 49
suffering, 35, 40, 58, 96, 130
"Sur le chemin de la Mort," 66
Surrealism, 16, 22, 23, 123

"Télégramme de Dakar," 66
"tête sort du mur, Une," 59
"Têtes," 81
"Thin Man, The," 127
"Toujours se débattant," 103
"Tout Petit Cheval, Un," 59, 61
Tranches de savoir suivi du Secret de la situation politique, 19, 99, 101

travel: real, 16, 17, 25-26, 70, 71, 74; imaginary, 64, 70-71, 101
Trois Nuits, 43, 44, 136

"Vacances," 115, 116
Vents et poussières, 19, 115-16, 120, 128
"Vents et poussières," 115
Vers la complétude, 19, 117, 119-20, 128
"Vers la sérénité," 52
Vie dans les plis, La, 93, 94-98, 106
Vie de chien, Une, 33, 34-36, 37
"Vie double, La," 87
"Vieillesse," 66-67
Vieillesse de Pollagoras, 98
"Villes mouvantes," 25-26
"Vision," 59, 60
"Vision de Plume," 43-44
"Vitesse et tempo," 107
"Voilà comment elle est," 103
"Voix," 88
"Voyage difficile, Le," 115, 116
Voyage en Grande Garabagne, 17, 18, 70, 72, 73-74, 75

"Yantra," 128-29
"Yeux, Les," 37